Praise fo

How I Came Into My Inheritance

"A piercingly funny book . . . unsentimental, breezy, blunt."
　　　　　　　　　　　　　　　　　　　　　　　　—Time

"Readers who relish the truth—served straight up, 120 proof—will be intoxicated by Gallagher's book and will accept her inheritance as their own."　　*—The New York Times Book Review*

"Ms. Gallagher's got brains, guts, talent, insight and a heart the size of the Ukraine."　　　　　　*—The New York Observer*

"A book that made me rejoice—there's no other word for it—in the perfect rightness of its tone and the hard-won compassion of its vision."　　　　　　　　　　　　—ALICE MUNRO

"Hilarious and alarming."　　*—Los Angeles Times Book Review*

"Throughout Gallagher's charming and touching memoir, there runs a wonderful voice: distinctly urbane, mercifully whine-free, and delighting in the details."　　　　　　　　*—Vogue*

"A tragicomic family saga with the stylish flourishes of a novel."
　　　　　　　　　　　　　　　　　　—Baltimore *Sun*

"There is not a word wasted. . . . Written with great, backhanded affection for the lost world in which she grew up."
　　　　　　　　　　　　　　　　　—The New York Times

Strangers in the House

"Charming, intelligent, and funny . . . Gallagher has a kind of simple and unfaltering grace in her prose style that you come to imagine matches a skill she has developed for living, cramming in so much with a kind of ease, never losing her balance or her sense of wry observation and self-possession."
—*O: The Oprah Magazine*

"These stories are clearly based in actual experience, yet they are crafted and illustrated works of art. . . . [Gallagher] is honest and funny about subjects usually treated with temerity, timidity, and shame." —*Boston Sunday Globe*

"So lively, so original, so readerly without being 'folksy,' so writerly without being 'bookish' . . . Gallagher's tales weave themselves into poetic romance." —*Bookforum*

"Gallagher captures moments of intensity, of change and kinetic energy." —*Los Angeles Times*

"A sharp picture of life on the edge of New York's literary world in the late twentieth century." —*The New Yorker*

"Wry, intelligent, unsparing, ironic, truthful, Gallagher is the most moreish of writers. . . . One of those addictions you would happily indulge to the point of death." —*The Guardian*

"The art of the essay perfected." —*Booklist*

LIFE STORIES

LIFE STORIES

How I Came Into My Inheritance

&

Strangers in the House

DOROTHY GALLAGHER

RANDOM HOUSE TRADE PAPERBACKS

NEW YORK

A Random House Trade Paperback Original

Published in the United States by Random House, an imprint of
The Random House Publishing Group, a division of
Random House, Inc., New York.

RANDOM HOUSE TRADE PAPERBACKS and colophon
are trademarks of Random House, Inc.

How I Came Into My Inheritance was originally published in hardcover
in the United States by Random House, an imprint of The Random House
Publishing Group, a division of Random House, Inc., in 2001.

Strangers in the House was originally published in hardcover
in the United States by Random House, an imprint of The Random House
Publishing Group, a division of Random House, Inc., in 2006.

Portions of this book were originally published, some in a different form,
in *The New York Times Book Review*, *Raritan*, Areté (England), *Epoch*, *Grand
Street*, *The New York Times Magazine*, and *More*.

Grateful acknowledgment is made to Harcourt, Inc. for permission
to reprint an an excerpt from "List" and an excerpt from "Among the Multitudes"
from *Monologue of a Dog* by Wisława Szymborska, copyright © 2002 by Wisława
Szymborska, English translation copyright © 2006 by Harcourt, Inc.
Reprinted by permission of Harcourt, Inc.

ISBN 978-0-8129-7265-8

Library of Congress Cataloging-in-Publication Data

Gallagher, Dorothy.
[How I came into my inheritance]
Life stories / Dorothy Gallagher.
p. cm.
First work originally published: 2001; 2nd work originally published: 2006.
ISBN 978-0-8129-7265-8
1. Gallagher, Dorothy. 2. New York (N.Y.)—Biography. I. Gallagher, Dorothy.
Strangers in the house. II. Title. III. Title: Strangers in the house.

CT275.G248A3 2007
974.7'1043092—dc22 [B] 2006102806

Printed in the United States of America

www.atrandom.com

2 4 6 8 9 7 5 3 1

To Ben

FOREWORD

Daniel Mendelsohn

Let me begin with a warning: There's one thing in the pages you're about to read about which Dorothy Gallagher is dead wrong. If you think this is a peculiar way to introduce a book that one loves, let me hasten to add that, having read these pages myself a number of times over the past five years or so, I'm pretty sure it's the only thing she gets wrong.

Anyway, it's a forgivable mistake. The passage I'm talking about comes in a chapter of *Strangers in the House* called "In the Vicinity of Art" (a title whose irony, as you discover when you get to the end of the chapter, manages to be both mordant and poignant: a not untypical combination here). In it, the author, recalling the disintegration of an old friendship, is describing the complicated awkwardness that comes with reading the work of a person you're close to:

Reading is reading; when you're reading something good there comes a moment when the physical experience of looking at print dissolves and the work takes you over; you're deep into a journey. But reading a friend's work can never quite offer that experience.

You'll see (as she might write, in that casual, deceptively confiding way she has) where I'm going with this. To be sure, the description of what it's like to get absorbed in a book is characteristically acute: a clear and unsentimental account of an experience that's actually deeply emotional. (She does that a lot.) But the stuff about never having that experience with a friend's work is sheer bunk. I speak from experience: Dorothy Gallagher happens to be a friend of mine, and every time I pick up the two volumes of these "life stories," they take me over. I'm deep into a journey.

What makes this particularly remarkable is that, with perhaps two exceptions, the journeys you're about to embark on aren't the kind you read about in travel magazines: They won't take you to exotic locations, you won't encounter strange tribes. (Well.) The autobiographical trajectory that's mapped in *How I Came Into My Inheritance* and *Strangers in the House* is, in a certain way, a modest one—even, at first glance, a relatively familiar one. A daughter of Russian Jewish immigrants grows up in and around New York City and observes, from the already wary perspective of the gifted child, some colorful older relatives. There is the indulgent Stalinist mother ("Who said Trotsky was assassinated, darling?"). There is the stolid aunt who sells lingerie to hookers; other aunts and uncles, too, her mother's siblings, with their smothering affections, rivalries, secrets. There is a fervently Communist cousin who leaves an autobiography that, not unlike the one you're about to be reading, leaves you confused about where the world-historical leaves off and the personal begins. "I was all my life on the side of the underprivileged," Cousin Meyer wrote. "For a little while I had happiness in love."

The young daughter of this intense Jewish family grows up a little more and, she confides, makes some mistakes: There are tellingly abbreviated references to marriages that didn't work out, scary accounts of abortions in the bad old days, amusing anecdotes about early writing gigs at gossip magazines, wry accounts of the kind of privations all young writers know too well. Not all of them were financial. "Who'd hire a good-for-nothing like you, anyway?" the author's father muses rhetorically at one point. (Early on in *How I Came Into My Inheritance*, the author mentions having "abandoned" her father's ashes at a funeral parlor, and then remarks, with a characteristic blend of breeziness and toughness, that "abandoned" is "*not* too strong a word": You don't doubt it, or her, for a minute.) If lines like that are hard for us to read, they were also necessary for Gallagher to hear. At least part of the inheritance to which she so movingly lays claim in the first of these two volumes was her titanic, difficult father's ferocity of mind—and also her gentle mother's shrewd, perhaps self-protective guilelessness. That combination is surely what gave the author her distinctive voice, with its characteristic one-two punch, the sweetly seductive confidence culminating in some hard-headed (but never -hearted) *apercu*. It's certainly what makes the telling of these life stories at once so bracing and so winning—what elevates Gallagher's autobiography above so many others.

The young woman eventually finds her footing. She has some nice successes in her career, about which she somehow knows how to gloat appealingly, if that's not too much of an oxymoron ("a full-page, glowing—if I may say so—review in the *Times Book Review*": It's the "if I may say so" that makes you love her). She finds the right husband (the editor and writer Ben Sonnenberg); finds herself moving more easily in the world. She has the kind of experiences you tend to have as an adult, experiences that are, like so much of adult life, at once terribly dramatic and yet almost reassuringly mundane: friendships eagerly embarked on and then mysteriously yet inexorably screwed up (*not* too strong a word), oddly passionate acquaintances with people whose exotic glamour first flatters and then exposes our own vanities—which, quite typically here, Gallagher is only too happy to autopsy. (Just why was it so important to know "Foucault's Last Lover"?) She buries both her parents. Her husband becomes chronically, gravely ill. The latter is a deep and delicate subject—by far the most "dramatic" part of Gallagher's life—that the author manages to finesse, in an essay called "Stay," by twining her brief but pungent account of his physical decline with the story of a beloved dog's demise. If the importation of Harry the dog seems like a sentimental out—seems to smack of Gallagher's maternal inheritance—never fear: The father's voice is there, too, snapping us back to another kind of reality:

> "This dog is a nightmare," I'd say to Ben. "He's ruining my life." Honestly? Sometimes I wasn't sure if it was Harry I meant.

Like a great cocktail, Gallagher's prose—no, her *thought*—goes down smoothly, but can conceal a potent kick.

You could, in fact, say that of the structure of the book as a whole. I made the claim earlier that the life story you get in these pages is, in many if certainly not all ways, unexceptional for a certain kind of woman born into a certain kind of family at a certain moment in the history of American culture; and I hope that the snippets I've quoted above will have made it clear that what gives that story great and memorable distinction is the consciousness of the person who lived it, as expressed in an idiosyncratic and winning voice: self-aware without being self-involved, casual without being cute, acerbic—about herself as much as about others—without being acidic, and above all, deeply feeling without descending into sentimentality. These qualities are desperately needed in autobiographical writing just now, when so much writing about the self hovers not far above the level of self-help books, when self-exposure passes so often for self-examination.

But there are (as I also said earlier) a couple of exceptions to my claim that the journeys on which Gallagher takes you aren't exotic. Each of the two volumes of her autobiographical prose, now gathered within the covers of this book, ends very self-consciously with a real journey, one that very purposefully takes us out of the inevitably narrow universe that is one's own life and forces us to consider the larger world; and indeed acknowledges, with a tart if only implied self-awareness, the writer's own small place in it. *How I Came Into My Inheritance* concludes, movingly, with the author traveling to Romania, where at one point she stands looking over the border into Ukraine, "as close as I was ever going to get," she writes, to her parents' and aunts' and uncles' homeland. It's a culminating moment—inevitably characterized, as so much in this author's work is, by a complicated fusion of regret and satisfaction, of an intelligent awareness of the necessity of pain in life, and the equal necessity of pleasure—in which she achieves a kind of reconciliation, however fleeting, with the unquiet ghosts of her long-dead older relatives, those cranky old Jews with whom she began her story. She tells us that at that moment, quite fittingly, "grief slipped away."

But no such escape from grief is possible in the final section of *Strangers in the House*, where again the author suddenly, devastatingly pulls back for the wide-angle shot. Contrary to her own earlier expectations, Gallagher now finds herself in the very place she'd never expected to reach: Ukraine, and then Russia. She's traveled there to track down and help a distant cousin—the granddaughter of her own mother's elder sister, who had been the only one of her mother's siblings who stayed behind when the rest came to America, a migration that gave us the characters and the stories we know so well from *How I Came Into My Inheritance*. In Ukraine, in Russia, she—and we—are made suddenly and crushingly aware that the life she's lived so richly, in all its vibrant, self-conscious, citrusy details, the neuroses and failures that she's had the good sense not to make too much of (although of course we understand that such is the substance of most peoples' lives)—that this life could have been so very much worse. The impoverished, toothless cousin she meets, the sole survivor of a family decimated by Hitler, Stalin, and time itself, and now pathetically eager to see the famous Dorothy from America, is like a stark figure from a dreadful parable: the figure, say, of History—and from which, it turns out, Gallagher had been happily shielded:

> Did she see my great, good, pure dumb luck? Did she see that my road had always been clear and open before me? Why didn't *I* know that?

The answer, of course, is one to which *Life Stories* itself furnishes a tart but humane reply: because we're living our own lives too much to see the bigger picture; and because it's our lives, there's nothing—and everything—wrong with that myopia. It's a heartrending ending to a strangely, quietly powerful book.

A final word about dumb luck. I began by mentioning the awkwardness that can come with being personally connected to the writing whose work you happen to be reading; and I suspect you think I've been saying all these nice things about Dorothy's book because she's a friend of mine. But the truth is that I didn't know Dorothy when I first read and loved these pages. That was in 2001, when *How I Came Into My Inheritance* was first published; I read it because I was reviewing it, and it's a matter of record that the review I then published was as glowing (if I do say so myself) as what you're reading here. It was only afterward that I met her, and liked her, and we became friends. I know from experience that it's not necessarily the case that the person who writes a book that you love turns out to be someone you want to be *friends* with. I suspect that everyone who reads this book will want to know Dorothy, too; it's just unlikely that all of them will get to have her as a friend. How lucky was I?

CONTENTS

HOW I CAME INTO
MY INHERITANCE

—

Memory at last has what it sought.
My mother has been found, my father
  glimpsed.
I dreamed up for them a table, two chairs.
They sat down...

—Wisława Szymborska

HOW I CAME INTO
MY INHERITANCE

—

After my mother broke her hip, I put her in a nursing home.

"You want to put me here?" she said.

The woman was certified senile, but she still knew how to push my buttons. Not that she didn't have reason to worry; had I listened when she'd begged me "Darling, please, please don't do anything to hurt Daddy. It will kill him . . ."?

I swear, what I did, it wasn't just for the money.

You know that tone people take about old age? The stuff about dignity and wisdom and how old people (pardon me for saying *old*) should be allowed to make their own decisions. Allowed! My father treated nicely reasoned arguments like mosquitoes. As for dignity, let's pass over the question of bodily wastes for the moment; let's suppose that the chronologically challenged father of one such pious person decided to torture and starve his or her chronologically challenged mother. ("So she falls! She'll lie there till she gets up! . . . What does she need orange juice for? If she's thirsty she'll drink water!") And not only that, but also gives away practically all that person's inheritance to a crook. Do you think you might see any revisionism in attitude then?

Until the day I took him to court and the judge laid down the law, nobody, but nobody, interfered with my father. I mean, he was awesome. For instance, he owned this slum building. It was filled with some characters you wouldn't want to meet in broad daylight on a busy street. The tenants didn't pay rent, welfare paid the rent. But welfare didn't pay *exactly* as much as my father was legally entitled to. So every month, even when he was up in his late eighties, he'd get in his car and drive over to that building, haul himself up the stairs, bang his cane on every door, and demand his five or ten dollars. He got it. Nobody laid a finger on him. Nobody even slammed the door in his face. And the only way you could tell he might be even a little bit nervous was that he left his motor running. And the *car* was never stolen!

It wasn't easy to tell when my father began to lose his marbles, because he'd always been such a headstrong summabitch, as he called everyone who had a slightly different idea. But the winter he was ninety he took out the water heater. That was a clue. I went up there one day—they lived about sixty miles upstate in this house they'd lived in forever. Now, the house should have been my first clue. I knew that house. I grew up there. If ever there was a homemade house, that was it. My father built it all around us. First we were living in two rooms, then three; nine by the time he got finished, the rooms all stuck on in unexpected places, connected by closets you walked through to get to other rooms, short dark corridors and twisting staircases. He never got tired of making new rooms. When I was a kid I thought he had made the world. Like once, we needed a shovel for the woodstove. My father took a metal ice tray, cut off one end, rounded it, put a hole in the other end, and stuck a bit of pipe in. *Voilà!* I idolized that man.

And now the house was a wreck: jury-rigged electrical cords you tripped over, water dripping from the roof, buckets on the floor, smells of accumulated filth. I'd piss in my pants before I'd go into the bathroom. But the thing is, I still believed in my father; he'd always taken care of everything. So when I'd say, "Daddy, there's a leak over Mama's bed. Let me find someone to fix the roof," and he'd say, "Don't you do anything, I'll take care of it," I'd think, Okay, I guess he knows what he's doing.

Or I might say, "I'll get somebody to clean the house."

"It's clean! Mama cleans!"

So I say, "Mama, when did you clean the house?" She says, dementedly, "You saw, I just swept out. You know it doesn't get so dirty in the country."

I say, "But it smells bad," and my father says, "It doesn't smell!" I'd think: He seems sure. I guess it's not so bad. And everything happened so gradually.

Anyway, I'd go up to see them once a week or so, and this one time I find my father is hacking up pieces of scrap wood.

"Daddy," I say. "What are you doing?"

He cackles. *Hee hee hee.* I'm not making fun of him. That's the way he sounds. "I took out the water heater," he says, and he's rubbing his hands together in glee. "I'm putting in a wood-fired heater."

"Why, Daddy?"

"We'll heat with wood. It's cheaper."

"But, *Daddy!*" I say, and that's all I say. I don't mention that the outside stairs to the basement are icy in winter. I don't remind him that he's ninety years old and he can hardly get up and down the stairs in good weather. I don't say that my mother's hands will crack and bleed doing dishes in cold water, or that bathing, which is a once-a-month affair at best now, will occur never. I say, "But, *Daddy!*" because I know if I say any more, he'll say, "It's not your *business!*" And I'd think: Well, I guess it's not my business. And the truth is I'm still scared of him.

My father is really something. Everybody says so: "That Izzy. He's really something." They mean he's a force of nature; he takes his course no matter what. If he doesn't know it, it's not worth knowing; if it's not done his way, it's done wrong; what he doesn't like reading isn't worth the paper. One time I gave him a book by this Nobel Prize winner. "Tell him to get another trade!" my father said, no discussion.

About a year after he took out the water heater, he was in the hospital for a month. How he made it out alive, I'll never know. "Ninety-one," the nurses said. "God bless him." He comes home with tubes sticking out of everything. A tube out of you-know-where for his urine, a tube from his gallbladder. I get a nurse to take care of him. Two days later he calls me up: "Get her out of here! Get her out!" So I tell the nurse she'd better leave and I run up on the train to empty his pee bag and his bile bag. I got his *bile* on my *hands!*

My mother is no help, of course. She can hardly keep on her own feet. She's falling down every five minutes. I say, "Daddy, we have to have help. You don't want a nurse, okay. But for Mama. She falls." I think maybe I'll get around him that way.

"She doesn't fall!"

"I don't fall," my mother says. "When do I fall?"

"Mama! I just picked you up! Daddy, you saw! I just picked her up."

"So *I'll* pick her up."

We're sitting on the porch. My mother gets up. She thinks she's going to the kitchen to make lunch. She hasn't cooked anything for two years. *I* bring the food. She takes two steps, and falls down. My father says, "Watch!" He inches his chair closer to her and sticks out his cane.

"Belle! Grab the cane!"

The woman doesn't know what's going on, she only knows the master of the universe has spoken. She grabs the cane. "Get up!" he orders, and she tries to haul herself up. It takes about five minutes, with him desperately trying to hold the cane steady against her weight without falling out of his chair.

She's up! My father looks triumphant: "See!"

Right away she falls down again. This time he pretends he doesn't notice. He thinks he can get away with it because, on top of everything else, he's just about blind.

By now I'm really frantic. What am I supposed to do about this situation? I go to see some social-service people: Look, I say, my father's blind, he's been in the hospital three times with congestive heart failure and kidney failure, my mother's in really bad shape. I'm rushing up there every five minutes because there's another crisis, my father's a regular Collier brother, he's got plenty of money but he won't spend money for food, I got Meals-on-Wheels to come and he starts waving his cane around and yelling at them to get off his property, he won't have a nurse or even someone to clean up, he fires everybody I hire, they have no hot water, he keeps the thermostat below sixty in winter. If they die there'll be a headline in the paper: STARVING OLD COUPLE EATEN BY RATS: MILLION DOLLARS FOUND IN MATTRESS.

I don't know how many social-service types I told this story to. And in case they thought I was exaggerating, I had documentary evidence.

This house is very dangerous to work in. The man is a very bad man I think he's mad. When he don't want you around he say you steals his money. Before you working here ask around the neighborhood and everyone will say it's the truth. The woman is very nice and quite but him? It's the worst human being I've ever come across. Be careful and think first before you accept the job. His wife is very sick. She suffers with a fainting spell. When you getting this job he don't tell you this. He also is suffering from some disease. The food you have to cook turns you off, its like YAK. His daughter lives in the city. She's a very nice person but he treats her bad.

I don't know which of the aides my father fired wrote this note. Not the one who refused to masturbate him, or she would have mentioned it. But what did I get from the helping professions? I got a lot of Tsk tsk, really nothing we can do if your father refuses help, he has rights.

"What about my mother's rights?" I ask.

"I don't suppose you could move in yourself, dear?"

Probably you're wondering the same thing. Why don't I just move in with them? It's not that I didn't think about it. I thought about it every day. "If you're so worried about Mama, *you* take care of her!" my father once yelled at me. And it was getting so I was up there every other day, it was getting so I had no life but them, thought of nothing but them. But I couldn't move in. Could not. Okay, would not.

That's what this shrink I went to said. She said it was my choice. She said maybe I wanted my father to yell Uncle (I'm paraphrasing here), to say, Okay, kid, you were right, I was wrong, take over. Maybe so. But the way it felt to me was I *had* to go home every night. I *had* to take a breath that didn't smell of rot. I *had* to sleep in my own bed. If it had been just my mother, if I had known everything that was going on . . .

When I say "everything that was going on," I'm talking about the million dollars I thought was in the mattress. There wasn't any money in the mattress. My father, who, when I *plead* with him to get some help in the house, wails, "All my little savings will be gone!" had taken his hard-earned money, saved from a lifetime of work parking cars and pumping gas, not to mention extreme parsimony, and was giving it to some guy who promised to triple it.

By parsimony, I mean that when I was a kid this is how I learned to make a phone call: First you went to the telephone booth at the corner candy store. You dialed the operator for free, told her you'd been connected with a wrong number. In those innocent days the operator would return a nickel she believed to be your nickel and then connect you with the number you wanted. That's how my mother did it, that's how I did it, and that's one way the nickels added up.

The guy who was getting my father to give him his money

was some kind of genius. I don't mean that he's intelligent or educated or well-read or anything. He's a genius in his speciality, which happens to be getting money out of people. I'll tell you what he reminds me of—one of those guys who marries women in every state, gets them to turn over all their money to him, and then disappears. Finally one of the women tracks him down. Instead of being arrested, he goes on *Geraldo!* Six women appear on the show with him and say they don't care what he did, they won't press charges, all they want is to have him back because each of them *knows* that *she's* the one he really loves.

Roy, that's his name. I start asking around and I hear a few things. So I mention them. "Daddy," I say. "Want to guess what I heard about Roy?"

"He was just a kid," my father says. "Got into a little trouble." He seems as proud of the guy as if he'd learned his ways at my father's knee.

"Daddy," I say. "I saw the guy's bankruptcy petition. He owes almost a million dollars. A quarter of that is *yours!*"

"That's not *your* business," my father says. "It's *my* business. It's *business*. These things happen in business."

Anyway, the way I first learned about Roy is that once a month my father and I sit down at the kitchen table. Under the light from one fluorescent bulb, which is all he allows in the ceiling fixture, we go over his bank statement. I call out every check. He tries to remember what it was for. Then, if he *can* remember, I check it off on the statement. So every month I'm seeing these checks, written in a strange handwriting but signed by my father's trembling hand at an extreme distance from the signature line. Checks are made out to building-supply companies, to lighting contractors, like that. And many of them are made out to this guy Roy. It's all adding up to a lot of money.

Finally I say: "Daddy. Who's this Roy?"

"We're in business!" he says.

"Oh gosh, you're in business, Daddy!" I do my best to sound delighted. How many ninety-three-year-old fathers choose this method of putting their affairs in order for their loved ones?

"What kind of business?"

"You wouldn't understand!"

"Daddy," I say, trying flattery. "Everybody says I got my brains from you. I *would* understand." Many wouldn't.

"We're putting up a development."

"Houses?"

"Twelve houses. Modulars. Roy's building the model."

"No kidding? He's your partner?"

"We have an arrangement."

"So when will these houses be finished?"

"A few years."

Don't think I don't realize that I'm faced with an ethical problem. This guy was a shark, that was clear enough. "Him!" said the local lawyers and businesspeople; everyone knew a story. But Roy understood certain things about my father. For instance, the greed at the heart of his parsimony, the same greed for life that makes old men hunch deep over their plates and shovel in the food. Roy flattered him; my father blushed like a girl when Roy praised his shrewdness. Roy promised he'd live forever and told him stories of ninety-nine-year-olds who ran the marathon. Roy promised him fabulous profits from their "development" that would materialize years in the future—years in my father's future. So what right did I have to interfere with my father's raison d'être? Or, as Roy says to me later on, when I *beg* him to use his influence to get yet another nurse's aide into the house, "A man's got a right to live the way a man wantsta live."

Summabitch, as my father would say.

At last I meet Roy. One day I go to the house, dragging bags of cooked food as usual. I always stop at the top of a small rise just before I get there. Standing on that hilltop, I can see my mother and father on the porch. What I actually see is a heap of rags bunched up on the mattress of the porch swing. That's my mother. My father is sitting on his wood-slatted metal chair, sort of rocking back and forth. Usually his radio is blaring Howard Stern or Bob Grant so loud I can hear it fifty yards away, but not today. Today I see he's talking to someone. Or rather, someone seems to be talking to him. Kneeling down in front of him in fact. Leaning toward him. Like he's begging or something. What is *this?*

"This is Roy," my father says.

Roy gets up off his knees when he sees me. He's not the least bit embarrassed. We take a good look at each other. I see a guy maybe in his late thirties, dark hair. He's not so tall, sort of stooped and round-shouldered, and he's got a little paunch. He sticks out his hand shyly and gives me a lit-tle smile, the kind where the teeth don't show. I can picture his smarmy face on a poster with the words WANTED and RE-WARD written above and below his photograph. That's what *I* see. What does he see? The fly in the ointment, no doubt.

"Your dad and I have a special relationship," he says. My father nods. "He's more like a dad to me than my own dad." My father beams. Then Roy remembers I have a "mom," too. He glances at the heap of rags on the swing and says, "And your mom, too."

"Mama," I say after Roy has taken my father to the "de-velopment" site. "Was Roy on his knees?"

"Yes," she says, very calmly.

"What was he doing?" I ask. I had no hope that anything had penetrated the fog of her stroke-damaged brain.

"You know. He wants money from Daddy. That one, what's his name? He's always asking Daddy for money." And then she says, asking my very own question, "Will there be anything left for us?"

"Daddy," I say to him soon after. "How do you feel about Roy?"

This is the kind of thing a woman asks a man she thinks has been cheating on her. There's no good news.

"Roy! He's like a son to me. He does more for me than a son would!" my father says to me.

I hear myself plead, "What about me, Daddy?" and before I can stop myself I'm reciting a list of my lifetime of devoted attentions.

"That's only natural," my father says. And then he looks straight at me with his bleary eyes. "Roy's got nothing to do with you! You want my money? You think *you* should have my money? It's *my* money. I'll do what I want with my money!"

So. Our lives had come down to this. Yes, I thought I should have his money. I thought it was only natural.

"Mama," I said. "I have to do something to stop Daddy from giving Roy all his money."

"Darling," she said. "Please, please don't do anything to hurt Daddy. It will kill him." A minute later she said, "It will kill me too."

I weighed their lives and mine, and I got a lawyer. Roy got my father a lawyer. My father's lawyer made a pretty good case for him; after all, he wasn't senile, just desperate to go on living. But the judge took one look at my ancient father, unable to stand in court, dressed in his filthy rags, and he made me my father's conservator. My father couldn't believe it. The look he gave me! *Bitter hatred.*

So what? Wasn't I *his* daughter?

"Mama," I said when we left the courthouse. "Do you understand what happened?"

"What did you do, darling?" she said. She put her hands over her face. *"Oh that I should live to see you and Daddy quarrel."*

Two weeks after the court ruling, my father was in the hospital. I went to the hospital every day. I had to. Roy was in a panic. All his plans were going down the tubes. Too bad I couldn't be in two places at once, because while I was at the hospital, Roy went to the house and took all the papers that showed how much money he owed my father. And then late one night he showed up at the hospital with a lawyer. They had a new will for my father to sign. I stopped them at the door.

"Daddy," I said. "Roy is here. Do you want to see him?"

I had to lean down, close to his mouth. He whispered, "Yes."

"He doesn't want to see you," I said to Roy.

"I don't believe you," Roy said. "Bitch," he said.

The lawyer said, "You have no right to stop us," but I stood in the doorway until they left. *Wasn't* I my father's daughter.

That night my father breathed his last. I sat in a chair next to his bed. I knew he was dying. The nurse said, "Shall I call the doctor?" I said, "No." I talked to my father. I urged him on. "It's okay, Daddy," I said. "Let go. Let go. It's been hard." I *wanted* to say "I love you, Daddy"; it came out "Mama loves you."

My mother let out such a cry when I told her. *"I'm all alone."* "You have me, Mama," I said. "Yes," she said. "That's everything." But when it came down to it, she was right.

Not long after my father died, my mother got out of bed in the middle of the night. She fell; her hip broke. In the hospital, coming out of the anesthesia, wild-eyed and flailing, she called *me* Mama. After that I had to put her in the nursing home.

The weeks passed. Every time I'd go to see her, she'd ask, "When will we go home?" She was crazy with anxiety.

"Daddy will worry," she'd say. "Oh, Daddy died? . . . I had an operation? It's a good thing Daddy's not here to be asking questions. He'd say, 'What did she need it for? How can we afford it?' . . . You think Daddy misses me? . . . So when will we go home?"

"Soon, Mama."

"How will we get there? Daddy has the car."

"We'll take a taxi, Mama."

"You always were a spender," she said.

Those promises I made to her: Sure, Daddy misses you, we'll go home soon, I'll see you tomorrow, you're not alone. Mama. I didn't think she'd remember from one minute to the next. But now I think she did remember. I think she figured out that there was no Daddy, she'd never go home, I wouldn't come tomorrow, she'd die among strangers. Early one snowy winter morning, almost exactly nine months after my father, she died. Among strangers.

In my mother's room at the nursing home I'd hung a picture that was taken just after I was born. I'm lying on a tiny cot surrounded by a cage of screening my father made to protect his baby daughter from insects. Our house is still a cottage. The lawn looks like a wild meadow. My mother leans over the cot, and oh god, what a fiercely tender gaze she gives me! My father, slightly out of focus, is sitting on a porch chair behind her, smiling at the scene. In the foreground is the trunk of the big old elm where my father built a swing for me.

Never mind that. I was telling you how I came into my inheritance.

NO ONE IN MY FAMILY

HAS EVER DIED OF LOVE

—

No one in my family has ever died of love.
What happened, happened, but nothing
myth-inspiring.

—Wisława Szymborska

I put my mother's ashes on the floor of the closet, right next to my shoes. I left them there from December until March. In March, a year after my father's death, I bestirred myself. I called the funeral parlor where I had abandoned (*not* too strong a word) his ashes. I wondered how long they kept uncollected cremains. Yes. Cremains. My father's cremains were still on the shelf, so I collected them, and one day in early spring I took a trip up to the house with my cousins and two boxes of cremains.

I'd found a buyer for the house, but it was still empty. In a few months the new owners will gut the place: Walls will come down as though they hadn't been inevitable, new rooms will erase the old ones, the Formica paneling, meant to resemble ash wood, will be junked, the ancient linoleum will be ripped up, light will pour in through new skylights, a deck will be built, God help us.

On the day I saw those wonders I had to knock on the door, but this day my key still worked. We walked through the dark, dismal rooms. Except for the sour smell of decay, everything was gone: clothes, furniture, books—none of it good enough for the Salvation Army—had been thrown into a dumpster by men wearing gloves and surgical masks. Here, under the kitchen windows, was where the table stood, covered with its stained plastic cloth; here, against the wall in the small room next to the kitchen (where I had spent my first year), the ancient pullout couch where my father, with no breath to climb the twisting, narrow stairs, spent his last year; down the narrow hallway, the bathroom. I thought I could still see smears of feces on the walls. And on the other side of the bathroom wall, my mother's bed had stood. Two months a widow and she got up at five o'clock one May morning, fell, broke her hip. That was the beginning of the end.

———

I was at the age to notice things. One thing I noticed was that when men came home in the evening, they kissed their wives. In the summertime, when fathers were away in the city all week, they kissed them longer.

"Why don't you and Daddy kiss?" I asked my mother.

"The kid wants to know why we don't kiss," my mother must have said.

"She wants a kiss, we'll kiss," my father must have said, because the next weekend they kissed, conspicuously, four eyes slipping sideways to see if I was noticing.

Oh, the falseness! Did they take me for a fool?

But I wasn't drawing any hard-and-fast conclusions. Wasn't my very existence proof of their love? And there was other evidence too. For instance, that snapshot of them taken before I was born, where they're standing in a meadow, young and darkly sexy, with their arms around each other's shoulders. And then there was the story of how she had left him and run away to Canada (she was always cagey about the reason; other women? callous treatment?) and he went all the way up to Quebec to bring her back. That was a good sign. And I had been there when he saved her life.

Yes, this happened in North Carolina. We were driving to Miami to visit my aunt Lily. My father wanted to make time, but it was so hot. *Please, please,* I begged, let's stop at a beach. We all went into the ocean. Now, my mother was no swimmer. At home she paddled about in the lake pretending to do the breaststroke, but if you dove under and looked, you could see that her feet were planted firmly on the bottom. My father did the breaststroke, too, but he knew how to swim. He could also float on his back and stick his feet up out of the water; I'd grab on to his toes and he'd tow me along.

So we'd been in the ocean for a while—me, my cousin Bobby, my father and mother—and when we came out to sit on the beach there were only three of us. Where was Mama? I looked around. She was out there, beyond the breakers, waving her arms in the most comical way. I have to admit it, I started to laugh. I couldn't stop laughing. My father hadn't seen her yet, and he didn't know *what* I was laughing at; I was laughing so hard I couldn't speak. I'm *sure* it was hysteria. I pointed. He dove into the breakers and pulled her in. She would have drowned, I know it, and at what point, I always wonder, would I have stopped laughing?

So what I decided was that even though there were no obvious signs of it—no kisses, no banter, no complicit looks between them; and, from his side, cold silences that sometimes lasted for weeks—that was just their way. There were things I was too young to understand.

Men and women, love and marriage: What a mystery at the center of life! It was invisible to my eye, but apparently, there was no power on earth to equal it. I knew that from soap operas on the radio and from movies. But even people I knew had been at its mercy. From what I heard, my mother's best friend, Rose, had been a happily married woman with a child when Albert appeared.

Albert was on the run. Nothing more romantic than a man on the run, particularly a man who looked like Albert, so handsome in the ascetic mode, all bones and severity, with a bushy crown of black hair, a strong, wiry body. Albert was a physical culturist, a follower of Bernarr MacFadden. He believed in exposing his naked body to cold, eating only nuts and grains, taking exercise every morning. And if this wasn't enough, he was a hero, hunted for his beliefs. With the Bureau of Investigation on his tail, Albert lit out from Philadelphia. Deportation or jail was in the offing, for he was, after all, a Communist. Arriving in Brooklyn, he hid out in the back room of my parents' delicatessen. And then Rose dropped by.

———

Rose is from Brailov, like my mother. She is a little older, and my mother, who tends to be worshipful, worships Rose. Rose is cultured and beautiful. Her hair, when she lets it loose, flows wild and black. Many men have been in love with her, and even after she was married, my own uncle-to-be, Noach (who will marry my aunt Frieda), was mad for her. As far as is known, Rose never gave him a tumble, or encouraged any other admirer, until Albert showed up.

"If you see Albert again, you'll never see your daughter," Rose's distraught husband threatens.

The threat didn't work, because here are Rose and Albert, whom I have known all my life, an old married couple living in the Bronx. To see them now, who would guess at the hot passion that had swept them away?

Would I ever manage to get in on this business? On buses and subways, I looked for the girls who wore engagement rings and wedding rings. They were only nine, ten years older than I was, but *they* were in on it. I stared at their work-weary, subway-riding faces for signs of the secret knowledge. They looked so . . . *ordinary,* and yet their initiation was publicly proclaimed by their rings, and sometimes by their big bellies. Weren't they embarrassed to have everyone *know* that they knew?

My father had given my mother no rings. That was their way. But they *knew.*

"Mama," I'd say. "Tell me how you and Daddy met. Tell me how you knew he was the one." She told me bits and pieces, here and there, until I had a story to tell myself.

———

This is how it begins. A small town called Brailov in a strange place called Ukraine. Some streets are cobblestone, others just dirt. When the rains come in the fall, everything turns to mud. There is a river nearby. In the distance are hills to which fields spread away. In summer the fields are carpeted with wildflowers. In winter the snow is waist-high and then, for many months, the inhabitants of the town huddle in their stone houses warmed by huge tiled stoves.

In this town, many years ago, my mother lived, and also a lovely young girl named Manya. Manya was tall and slender. She wore her thick brown hair in braids, which she wound in a coronet around her head. I can see her walking down the street, wearing an embroidered blouse and a fringed shawl wrapped around her shoulders; gold earrings sparkle as she walks. Manya is gay and charming and quick-witted. Everyone loves her, including the schoolteacher, who is a married man.

One cold, rainy morning in the late autumn of, say, 1912, Manya's parents awake to find their daughter's bed empty. In panic, they search all over town. It's a small town, but not that small.

Meanwhile, in another part of town, the schoolteacher's wife, who has waited all night for her husband to come home, opens her door to a knock. A neighbor hands her a note: *I have gone to America with Manya.* Running through the muddy streets, the poor wife wails her abandonment for all to hear. The town is scandalized for months.

Two years pass. My mother is now sixteen, and it is her turn to go to America, where her older sister, Lily, and brother, Oscar, are waiting for her. In Brooklyn the sisters find a room together. They work in sewing factories, sweatshops. Mama (still only Bella) is desperately homesick. She is haunted by the image of her own mother standing at the door of their house, arms outstretched, calling to her: *Mein kind, where are you going, my child?*

For many months Bella cries herself to sleep each night, grieving for her mother and the family she has left behind, for her language, her friends, her lost courage. She, who had been so lively and bold at home, is now fearful of everything. When she realizes that the other girls in the factory are making four dollars a week while she makes only $3.50, her sense of justice is outraged; she summons her courage. One day she waits until everyone has left the sewing loft for the night. She crosses the empty space, passing silent rows of sewing machines, hearing the echo of her footsteps. At last she stands before her boss's desk. He looks up from his ledger.

"What do you want?"

"Oh. I just wanted to say good night, Mr. Kominsky."

A year, two years go by, and Bella becomes reconciled to her new circumstances. She goes to Brighton Beach on her days off. Other girls from Brailov have emigrated: Rose, Tillie, Minnie. They study English at night school and go to free lectures. And Bella has the protection of Lily, who has always looked out for her. Gingerly, she enters into a new life.

One day, during the slow season in the garment industry, when both sisters had been laid off, Lily decides to go to Philadelphia to visit friends from home. She comes back to Brooklyn full of excitement.

"Guess who I saw in Philadelphia?" she says. "Manya!"

Not only had Lily seen Manya and the schoolteacher, but through them she had met an interesting fellow.

"Manya asked about you," she says to her sister. "Go see her. And you'll meet Isidore. See what you think about him." Lily couldn't stop talking about Isidore.

Bella is eager to see Manya again. She has often thought about her. Such romance! To give up everything for love, to be swept away by passion, never mind the scandal. Would she herself be equal to such a test? (What a romantic girl my mother is! Many years in the future, she will follow every detail of Ingrid Bergman's love affair with Rossellini.)

"I'll go to see Manya," she tells Lily, "but, please, I don't want to meet any strangers."

Once in Philadelphia, Bella is dismayed by the sour underside of romance. Manya has a baby, the schoolteacher is unfaithful, the house reeks of diapers and bitterness.

But soon young Isidore presents himself. He is not tall, but he is sturdy, with wavy, dark hair, a forceful nose, and gray eyes. In truth, his chin is a little weak, but only in profile. He is full of self-confidence; and a joker, a prankster, a real flirt. He has already flirted with redheaded Lily. Maybe she took him too seriously, because now he is flirting with the younger sister. Oh, *she* is a pretty girl, no doubt about it. Small and beautifully made. Big, sleepy hazel-green eyes, long black hair, a full mouth. Shy, but more than ready to laugh at his jokes.

Isidore takes Bella to the train station. "I'll write to you," he says. "I'll come to see you."

"Oh," says Bella, stricken with guilt. "Lily will be so happy to see you."

"I'm coming to see *you*," says Isidore. "Come closer. I have a secret to tell you."

Bella inclines her head. "You're a pretty girl," Isidore whispers. One day he'll say that to me. *Putty gull*, is what I hear.

A few weeks later Isidore is waiting outside Bella's factory. She's working in a glove factory now. He has bought her a present. A small wooden gilt-painted box; on the top, in ornate black lettering, are her initials, *BR*. There is a keyhole, and a key to open it. It is filled with chocolates. There is an augury here: Bella's initials will be the same when they marry; and she has a greedy love of sweets. She accepts the gift and enters Manya's country.

"I won't say anything to Lily," she says. "It will hurt her."

For two or three months they write secretly. Isidore writes to her in care of Tillie. He comes to Brooklyn again and stays with a friend. He and Bella take walks, ride the ferry. Bella lies to Lily.

While they are walking together on a cold winter day, Isidore takes Bella's hand and puts it in his pocket. They walk this way in silence for blocks. Later he writes to her: "Are you serious about me?"

"Would I have let you take my hand in that way if I weren't?" Bella answers. (She is not quite *that* innocent; a boy at home has written poems to her eyes; another fell in love with her on the boat to America.)

They begin to plan for the future. It is 1918. The country is at war. Isidore will enlist in the army; when he is discharged he will be eligible for citizenship. And then, when they marry, Bella will be a citizen, which will enable her to bring the rest of her family to America: two sisters, two brothers, a mother and father have fled Ukraine and are refugees in Bucharest.

It is time to tell Lily.

"So why do you think I would care?" Lily says. "He meant nothing to me." She is cold to her sister for a while, but it passes.

Isidore goes to France: Private Rosenbloom. His discharge papers show that he was at the scene of many battles: Avecourt, Pannes, the Meuse-Argonne, Ypres-Lys. He was not wounded, but he was very hungry, very cold, and all around him men were screaming in pain and dying. When he hears the news of the armistice, he deserts, wishing desperately to avoid the irony of being killed when the war is over.

"So, Rosenbloom," his captain says when he shows up at headquarters days behind the rest of his troop. "You're a dirty Jewish coward." He is threatened with court-martial, but it comes to nothing.

Through these long months, Bella has waited for the mail. A photograph of Isidore arrives, taken somewhere in France. He is very thin and wears a heavy backpack with a rifle slung from it. The inscription on the back reads *Your friend, Isidore*. Bella takes the picture to a photographer's studio and has a photograph of herself taken with Isidore inserted, floating in a dream circle above her head. "Thinking of you," she writes on the back.

A year after his enlistment, Isidore returns to Fort Dix. He has lost thirty pounds. People who knew him before he went to war say that he is a changed man. What has happened to him? Was he gassed? Have the scenes of war embittered him beyond repair? He never talks about it. "What difference does it make?" he says when Bella asks him a question. He is irritable, impatient, angry.

"Don't marry him," says Lily to Bella.

Lily is still jealous, Bella thinks. And, woman-like, she believes she can restore him. Her hand is still in his pocket. It is 1920 when they marry. He is twenty-five, she is twenty-two.

—

It had been more than a week since I'd seen my mother. I kept meaning to go up to the nursing home. It was a pain in the neck, really. The place was all the way up in the Bronx, and by the time I got there and back, a whole day was gone. In the beginning I'd go three times a week, then twice. Each time my mother saw me, she smiled with such joy. "How did you find me, darling?"

Rose was in the same nursing home. Albert had died. When the weather was nice, I took them both out to the patio. They sat side by side in their wheelchairs, not speaking, holding hands.

But now it was December and wouldn't you know it! On the very day I planned to go to the Bronx, there was a huge snowstorm, a northeaster that shut the city down. I had to wait another two days until transportation was back on schedule.

I took a subway that becomes an elevated as it reaches the Bronx. The snow was still white on the ground and on the roofs of the buildings. The dingy Bronx was incandescent. I got off near the end of the line and walked up the long hill to the nursing home. I was thinking about my mother's greeting: her smile, joyful, without reproach, despite my long absence; her invariable question: "But, darling, how did you find me?" My answer: "I'll always find you, Mama."

At the reception desk, I signed the register. The receptionist glanced up. Did a double take.

"Who are you here to see?"

"My mother." What was this? He knew who I was!

"Didn't anyone call you?"

"No. What about?"

My heart was beating. I knew. I *knew.* "What?" I cried. "Tell me, tell me. What! Tell me!"

They took me into a small room. The doctor came. There weren't many details. The night before, she'd vomited after dinner, but at seven in the morning she'd been awake, seemed all right. At eight, when they brought her breakfast, she was dead.

"You're not alone, Mama," I'd told her. "You have me."

"Oh yes," she had said. "That's everything."

They let me see her. She was in her room. It was very cold. The window had been opened wide to stanch the smell of death. Her mouth was open. Someone had closed her eyes. They had wrapped her in a large green plastic bag. They had attached a tag to her toe. They shouldn't have done that.

—

Why was I so afraid they would abandon me? They were always there. Never even a baby-sitter. Yet on winter nights in our city apartment, I was unable to fall asleep until I cracked open my bedroom door. Was the light burning in the kitchen? Was the radio playing? Yes. They hadn't gone. On summer nights my fears evaporated as they sat on the porch, all of them, just outside my room. I lay in bed listening to the murmur of voices, my mother's soft laugh, her "*Shhh, the kid is sleeping,*" my aunt Lily's sharp remarks, the men's monosyllabic conversation, the occasional flare of a match, the creaking of the porch swing. A little way off, on the road, I could see the beams from our neighbors' flashlights moving erratically, like extraterrestrial lights. The stars. The smell of summer. My family, my mother, my father. The mystery at the center of life that held them for seventy-two years.

—

We went outside, my cousins and I, and buried the cremains a few yards from the porch.

NO

—

Why do you always say no, darling?" my
mother used to say. "Someday you'll thank
me: Practice the piano . . . don't leave anything on your plate . . . work for half an
hour on your handwriting . . . you need a
tutor for math . . . make the revolution . . ."

—

Here we are, Mama and I, on the lawn outside
our bungalow at the end of a hot, still after-

noon in the second summer of war, face-to-face on the green double glider. (I buried her ashes just about where the glider stood.) Mama is sitting, and I am standing between her knees. Over her shoulder, through the mesh of the screen door into the kitchen, I see my plump aunt Frieda standing at the stove. (In her middle age she will be killed by a runaway car.) To my left, on the porch, my bossy aunt Lily, always a bit sickly, is napping on the swing. (She will live to her dotage and beyond.)

At this moment Mama and I, so often at odds, are in thrilling mutuality. She is painting my face. With her lipstick (Tangee Flame), she makes my mouth feel as heavy as honey. She makes red circles on my cheeks, dusts my nose with powder, ties a flower-printed kerchief over my braids, and holds up the mirror. *Behold!* From memory, she has drawn a Russian peasant maiden. In an hour or two my mother and aunts will watch proudly from the audience, and I, on the stage of the day camp, will swing a wooden scythe and sing "Meadowlands" to celebrate the glory of the Soviet people as they turn the Fascist tide.

And here we all are again, a couple of years later, August, the last summer of war. I am in the bathroom, thrilled at the sight of my first menstrual blood; only ten years old, but I know what's happening. I run to the kitchen to tell Mama.

She claps her hands. *Mazel tov!* she cries, and turns to tell my aunts, and my uncles too. Everyone congratulates me. Soon a neighbor comes to our door. *Mazel tov!* he calls. *How does he know?* But his congratulations are for the day's headlines: Russia has entered the war against Japan. History, on two fronts!

When I ask my mother a question about Russia, she says quite severely: "So why do you call it Russia, darling? It's the Soviet Union." Yes, yes I knew that, but I get confused. If I asked, "Where were you born, Mama?" she'd say, "You know where I was born, darling. In Russia." Russian was the language in which she and her sisters told their secrets; Russia—or at least a shtetl in Ukraine—was my heritage. The difference seemed to be that while the Russia of my mother's youth was hell on earth, the Soviet Union is the hope of the world.

The ramifications of this Russian/Soviet business radiated through my life. My very name, the "D" of it, honored Georgi Dimitrov, Bulgarian Communist, Comintern leader, hero of the Reichstag trial, the man who brought us the news of the Popular Front. My heart soared to the Red Army Chorus. I knew all the words to "Ballad for Americans," "Meadowlands," "The Banks Are Made of Marble," "The Four Insurgent Generals" before I knew my ABC's. I was in love with Sonny Speisman, who delivered the *Daily Worker* to our house every summer morning; then I was in love with Ernie Lieberman, who played the guitar. Handsome Ernie with the tight brown curls—with his head thrown back, he aimed his sweet tenor at the ceiling: *There once was a Union Maid/Who never was afraid/Of goons and ginks and company finks/And deputy sheriffs who made the raid.* Who was it who said: Beware the movement that makes its own music? Even today the opening notes from any one of those songs will sweep me away. (As for Ernie, decades later I recognized him on the checkout line at Zabar's; to general amusement, I call out, "Ernie! I loved you more than life itself!" He mouths, "Who are *you*?")

Anyway, this is what I take in with my mother's milk, but I am an ignorant, uninstructed child. "Trotskyite" is a well-known curse, but what does it mean? I don't even know that there was such a *person* as Trotsky. It is all as arcane as sex.

Actually, information about sex is easier to come by. From Nina, for example, one of three sisters, who comes running to me and her youngest sister, Irene. "I found prophylactics in the drawer on Daddy's side of the bed."

Irene and I look blank.

"Stupid! The man uses them when they don't want to have a baby." Nina is filled with disgust. "You'd think *three times* would have been *enough* for them!"

Without the picture on the jigsaw-puzzle box, how do you know what the pieces mean? When I think I have an inkling, I test my mother.

"Mama, what's rape?"

"Oh," she says. "It's when a boy kisses a girl and she doesn't want him to."

Is that *all*?

I listen when adults talk. I pick up words and phrases and sentences. I hear "Bolshevik," and "Stalin," and "the Party," and "class struggle," pronounced with reverence. I hear "Trotskyite," and "objectively an agent of Fascism," and "reactionary," and "class enemies" pronounced hatefully. Sometimes people who appeared in earlier conversations as "comrades" become "right-wing deviationists." My mother's cousin Sylvia explains why she will not be going to medical school after all: "They think I can do better work organizing."

Who are *they*?

"What are we, Mama?"

"We're Jewish, darling."

"No, I mean are we Democrats or Republicans?"

"You could say we're progressives."

Is that *it*?

I *love* this place where we spend our summers, and my winter school vacations too. We have an outhouse, no run-

ning water, a woodstove. My father, who can do anything,
built this house. My real life happens here, sixty miles upstate, at this colony for "Workers and Professionals Only,"
as it advertises itself, meaning: Nobody is allowed who
employs—read "exploits"—labor. (There was a small busi-
nessman who misrepresented himself as a worker. He was
expelled when it was discovered that he had three employees
who were on strike.)

But from September through June, when, during the
1940s, we lived at the upper edge of Harlem, my real identity goes into hiding. We still read the *Daily Worker*, but now
I have to walk blocks to buy it at a distant newsstand and
spend an extra nickel for the *New York Post* to wrap it in for
the dangerous walk back home. When Miss Ferguson, my
dreadful sixth-grade teacher, tells us to bring in the newspapers our parents read, I hesitate only between the *Post* and
P.M. and settle on the *Post* as the safer bet.

My classmates are Irish, Italian, Negro: *Americaaaaaan*,
as Paul Robeson sang in celebration of premature multicul-
turalism. On my block—167th Street, between Amsterdam
and Edgecombe Avenues—everyone is Italian until suddenly,
after a summer away, we return to find that all the Italians
have gone and everyone is Negro. At my school—a Gothic
fortress on Broadway and 168th Street—almost everyone is
some variety of Catholic—or Negro.

Now, I know the story of the Scottsboro Boys. I know that among the oppressed and exploited proletariat (with whom we are as one) the Negro people rank highest and are to be most esteemed. I have heard the talk about Jim Crow and The Negro Question and The Necessity to Root Out White Chauvinism. I have sung the songs of Leadbelly. But here's my problem: Negro children just don't like me. When I was three or four years old and we lived on Stebbins Avenue in the Bronx, my little playmate Shirley announced one day: "My mama says I can't play with you no more because you're white trash."

"Mama, Shirley says I'm white trash."

"That's just an expression, darling."

In fourth grade, May and Edna have the desks on either side of me. On a test day, May goes to the bathroom. An evil breeze blows her test paper to the floor. She comes back, sees her paper, and stares hard at me.

"What?" I whisper.

"You threw my paper on the floor!" she hisses.

"I didn't!"

"You did so. Fuck your mother."

What does this mean? Is it just an expression?

"Same to you," I say.

May and her four friends (her gang; I have no gang) circle me after school.

"She said 'fuck your mother,' " May explains.

I start to run. Edna sticks out her foot. I trip. My hands and knees are scraped raw. Someone shoves me, someone else hits me. I run and run until I run flat into a lady, who puts herself between me and my pursuers and takes me home.

And I tell no one.

"Oh! What *happened* to you?" Mama says.

"I fell, Mama."

"Be more careful, darling."

I just have this feeling that Mama won't take my side, that ideology—though I am years from knowing this word—will interfere with simple justice. I believe that, somehow, Mama will make it my fault. Suppose I had told her the story: the test paper blown to the floor, the words exchanged, etc. I swear she would have said something like: "Darling, you must work to eradicate white chauvinism in yourself; as the vanguard of the working class, we must show the Negro masses how to take their place among the international pro-letariat."

If you think I'm laying it on too thick, listen to this: I spent my thirteenth and fourteenth summers at Camp Wochica (Workers' Childrens' Camp, in case you thought it was your standard inauthentic Indian name). Our camp song was sung to the tune of "Oh Moscow Mine," and our project was to dig a new cesspool for the camp. (Talk about the theory of surplus value!) I learned to smoke cigarettes during those summers, to wield a shovel, and gratefully, with Karl and Anatole, I learned more about sex. For the same money I had instruction in detecting hidden manifestations of white chauvinism.

Once a week, more often if circumstances demanded, we were subjected to sessions of self-criticism so that we might admit to errors in our behavior, and have the opportunity to point out errors in the behavior of our fellow campers. These sessions were led by our counselor, Elsie, in a sort of mini-trial format designed to, as the not very catchy slogan went, "root out every manifestation of open or concealed white chauvinism in our ranks."

Elsie to an unwary camper: "Sasha! Did you offer Joan [Negro] a slice of watermelon?"

Sasha: "Well, yes, but we had watermelon for dessert that day . . ."

Elsie: "But Bernie reported that you passed Joan an *extra* slice. Do you admit this?"

Sasha: "She asked me . . ."

Elsie: "So! You blame Joan for her own oppression!"

Poor Joan burst into tears, maybe from embarrassment,

or maybe realizing at last the extent of her own oppression. I passed her a tissue.

Elsie: "And you! What right do you have to act as Joan's friend when you have *never* made a special effort to gain her friendship?"

You know what would have happened if I had made such an effort? *A transparent attempt to avoid charges of chauvinism!*

Time passed and I graduated into the Labor Youth League, successor to the Young Communist League. We met in a firetrap tenement on the Lower East Side. At one meeting I got into an argument with our leader, whom we called Rooster (long neck, bobbing Adam's apple). I can't remember what the argument was about: probably something about the wording of one of those jargon-filled leaflets we handed out on street corners to the working class, who (misled by False Consciousness) despised us. I sat in my chair in that cold, badly lit, dirty room, brooding on my grievances. I hated handing out those leaflets to passersby, who at best ignored my out-thrust arm and at worst snarled or even spat at me. I hated being monitored for deviations in thinking and, in turn, being a heresy hunter myself. I was at that moment in a dark, smoky room, and my life was feeling just as airless. I still didn't understand what Trotsky had done that was so horrible, for God's sake! I got up to leave the meeting.

"Sit down!" Rooster called. "A Negro comrade is speaking!"

I was sixteen. It was 1951. The Hollywood writers had been blacklisted; people had informed or refused to inform in front of HUAC; Alger Hiss had been convicted of perjury; the Rosenbergs had been arrested; my English teacher at Seward Park High School had been fired for subversive activities; family friends were being followed by the FBI, whose agents sometimes knocked on our door to try to ask my mother questions. For lack of anyone else to ask, I sometimes asked her questions myself.

"Mama, why did Stalin have Trotsky assassinated?"

"Who says he was assassinated, darling? Some deranged person killed him."

"Mama, why did Stalin sign the pact with Hitler?"

"That was a tactic, darling. To give the Soviet Union more time to prepare for the war."

"Mama, are the Rosenbergs Communists?"

"They're progressives, darling. They're being persecuted because they believe in justice for all people, and because they're Jews."

"Is Alger Hiss a Communist?"

"Of course not. He's a liberal person who's opposed to the warmongers."

"What about Whittaker Chambers? He says *he* was a Communist."

"He's a very sick man."

In this time of trouble, was I a rat leaving a sinking ship? Who was I, if not who I always had been? Who would my friends be? What would we talk about? How would I learn a new vocabulary? And *what* would replace the central mission of my life, to man the barricades when the revolution came?

———

A few months after my mother died, I dreamed we were together in a foreign country, hurrying along a path toward her childhood home. When we reached the house where she had been born, we found it deserted and derelict: wooden plank walls were splayed apart; the roof gaped; a few half-starved animals wandered around an overgrown yard. In dismay we started back toward the town, hoping to find someone who could tell us what had happened to the inhabitants of the house. The light began to fade. I saw that my mother had crossed the road. She was walking very quickly now, each step leaving me farther behind. I called to her to wait; I was in terror of being left alone in this strange country, where only she knew the language. Then it was pitch-dark. I could not see my mother anymore. I shouted, "Mama! Mama!" but she was gone.

Of course I was dreaming about my mother's death. I

was still grief-stricken and bereft. But when the sound of my own voice woke me, I knew in what country she had abandoned me.

And then I remembered that I had first abandoned her.

It was 1948, the year Henry Wallace ran for president. Mama and I were at Madison Square Garden. We were at the very top of the house, looking down on the brightly lit arena. Standing at the center of the stage was Vito Marcantonio, *our* congressman. Oh, he was a *wonderful* speaker, my mother always said, a fiery orator. That man knew how to work a crowd. And as he spoke, his feet stamping, his arms waving, his voice growing louder and more rhythmic as he approached the climax of his speech, the entire audience rose to its feet, chanting with him, roaring approval. And I was on my feet too, transported, at one with the crowd, melted into it, my voice its voice. I was lost.

And suddenly, without willing it, as the crowd still roared, I came to myself. I felt very cold. I looked at Mama, still on her feet, clapping, chanting. *Who was she* now? About Marcantonio, I thought: *He could tell us to do anything now, and we'd do it.* I was out of there. I was history.

No, I said. But not so Mama could hear.

COUSIN MEYER'S

AUTOBIOGRAPHY

—

When my cousin Meyer (twice removed) reached the age of eighty-seven, he committed suicide. His health was bad, his prospects grim, and everyone said he was a man who looked facts in the face. "You will need a car to attend to everything, so better drive here," he wrote to his daughter. "My door will be unlocked, get somebody to walk in with you. . . ." He gave instructions about his cremation, and about important papers "in the white tin box." Among these papers was a manuscript addressed "To Whom It May Concern."

—

I am a simple man. I am uneducated. Yet I lived long and kept my eyes open. In my youth I read books: Chernyshevsky, Bakunin, Lasalle. I formed opinions. From my readings and my experience of the world, I came to the conclusion that only the system of socialism could liberate mankind, because it would abolish the system of exploitation of man by man. Could it be that I was wrong? Of this I will never be convinced! After all, didn't I endure hardship? Didn't I struggle for my living while others profited from my misery? Yes, I had convictions. I stuck by my convictions.

Now. To begin at the beginning. I was born on March 4, 1893, in a cold, dark room in a small town called Brailov in the Ukraine. I never knew my father. He dropped dead when I was in the womb. My mother already had six children, and there was no milk in her breasts for me. How I cried with hunger when she held me to suckle those empty breasts! That I survived at all was a miracle. When I was eleven years old, my mother took me to the city of Zsmerkinka and left me there to work in a store of flour and grains, just for the price of my room and board. How cruel they were to me! I was still a child. I longed for my home and family. I cried from hunger and cold.

Poverty and hunger formed me. And history too. When I was a young boy in 1905, a revolution failed. There were many pogroms in our area. Once, when the Cossacks came, my mother put my sister in the stove. Still, we had some laughs. Every other Sunday we had a fair in Brailov. People made jokes: About Reb Mates, who was cross-eyed, we used to say that he looks on onions but buys potatoes. And I remember one Saturday night in summer when a group of us boys hired a boat and went rowing on the lake. We sang such songs! *Carry away my soul into the blue far distance.* It seems like only yesterday, the beautiful dreams of our promising youth. Who, *who* is still alive to remember that Saturday night!

One question I have always asked myself: Why do we not all agree and put our efforts to learn how to distribute the great wealth of our planet equally to all mankind? This world of ours would then become a paradise on earth!

Well, to go on. There was no future for a poor boy in Brailov, so I went to Odessa. My mother warned me of the bad women who walked the streets there: "I am your mother," she said. "It is my duty to warn you that you could get infected with a terrible disease. Your nose will fall down in small pieces. You might get blind. In the end it will reach your brain. You get insane and soon you die in terrible agonies." Believe me, I listened to my mother and never forgot her warning my whole time in Odessa.

When I was twenty years old, I went to America. This was just before the Great War broke out. I sailed on a dirty, miserable ship. Eighteen days later we saw land. It was like Moses seeing the land of Israel, except for the skyscrapers. Then my struggles really began: one job after another for a few pennies a week. I lived for a while with my cousin Mendel under the elevated in the Bronx. I got used to it. First I worked in a steam laundry, then I got a pushcart and sold remnants. What didn't I do in the land where gold was supposed to lie on the streets? The exploitation at that time in America was inhuman. There were no unions to protect workers.

And then we heard the great news! Czar Nicholas lost his throne and his head! Lenin and Trotsky made a victorious revolution! No more Capitalism! No more private property! We danced in the streets. But we knew their road would not be an easy one.

As if to celebrate this glorious event, my son was soon born. I was then working as a streetcar conductor, then I drove a milk wagon seven days a week. Always my wages stayed just a few pennies ahead of starvation. A few years later I had a daughter. I loved my son, but every father loves also to have a little girl. Such a beautiful little girl. Cheeks like two red roses, and big shining eyes.

It occurs to me that I forgot to put in that I got married. If I didn't mention this before, it's because the less said about it the better. My wife and I didn't get along. Whose fault was that? It was one of those things. A man isn't always lucky in his marriage. I loved a woman, but she was not my wife; I'll come to that. However, I did my best for my family. I had a chicken farm, and believe me I sweated blood there. My chickens froze to death one night and I was wiped out clean. Then I bought a grocery store that burned to the ground. I picked myself up and went on. What else could I do?

My children were growing up and I was proud of them. My boy and my girl were smart children. When the time came, I was able to put them through college. Even in the Depression, when people were on breadlines, I managed so we never went hungry. What happened to this greatest, richest land in the world? What happened to "a chicken in every pot"?

When my boy was fifteen, I decided to take a trip to my

old home to see my mother before she died. I also wanted to see the new system, the Soviet system. To tell you the truth, I also had a furtive hope to remain there and thus liberate myself from my very unhappy marriage.

Well, when I say that I went to the Ukraine in 1932, I don't have to tell you what I found. Stalin's collectivization. When I arrived in Brailov, the entire Jewish population was on the verge of total starvation. The Depression in America was nothing compared to it. My mother was emaciated, lifeless. I hardly recognized her. She was so weak she could not raise herself to greet me. *What happened to my mother? Where has her hearty humor gone?* She did not even have tears left in her eyes, they had dried out. And my sisters! My brothers! I had heard some rumors, but this I could not believe. I unpacked my suitcase, which I had filled with as much food as I could carry.

Where are the pots? I asked my mother. "Pots?" she said. "We have no pots. We sold the pots. What do we need pots for? We have nothing to cook."

That night in my old home I could not fall asleep. It looked to me like a nightmare. Outside my window I heard cats and dogs crying with hunger. The next morning I walked out to see once more my childhood place. What did I see? Abandoned horses, tiny like dogs, starving, all their ribs showing, standing motionless on the streets, full of sores, their eyes and their sores all covered with flies. The few people with enough strength to leave their houses walked slowly, aimlessly.

I asked myself the question: Must this be the terrible price that people had to pay to bring about a better society? I could not stay with my family more than three days. It would kill me. I had to leave them to their own fate. In my heart I said: Good-bye, my dear family; good-bye, my Russian friends. I wish you from the bottom of my heart great success in your hard task.

You see, we must always remember that the Soviet leaders were the first in the history of mankind who took upon themselves the great task of building a new society on communist principles. We will admit they made lots of mistakes. They were moving along unexplored paths. Even the Bible tells us that before God created this world of ours, there was darkness and disorder. I kept my faith. When people asked me, What about the sufferings and sacrifices of so many human beings? I have always been able to reply with confidence: After all, since the beginning of history, millions of people were killed in wars in the interests of kings and imperialist bandits. True, the Russian revolution came about with a terrible price in deaths and in sufferings—hunger and starvation. But it was all in the interests of the *people*. To end the dog-eat-dog system. It is too bad that this generation had to pay such a terrible price, but it was unavoidable. They did not die in vain; they fought to bring for their children a better life. Isn't this so? This I will believe until my dying day.

And even this terrible suffering grew pale next to the sufferings of the war. Of course I heard nothing from my family during the war. When it was all over, I wrote to my niece Lyuba to find out what had happened to my family. This is what she wrote to me:

I am worried that my letter will make you sick, dear uncle, but I can't bear it alone. Our town was occupied by the Germans in July 1942. There were four slaughterings in our town. The first was on the 12th of February, 1942. No more Papa, no more Mama, no brothers and sisters, no one. All three thousand Jews in Brailov were killed by the Nazi murderers. They declared my home *Judenrein*.

These things are beyond imagining. For many years I have had nightmares about the sufferings of my family. If only, if only I could have saved them, if I could have known. . . . If it counts against me in the reckoning of my life that I did not try to save them while it was still possible, so be it.

To change the subject for the better, there is another thing I must tell. On this trip I took to the Soviet Union in 1932, I met a girl on the boat. I was then thirty-nine years old, but I looked younger. She was twenty-nine, a social worker from Canada. A nice girl. I was the first man in her love life. I told her that I was a married man with two lovely children, but she did not care. She wanted to experience life, to enjoy herself. For two months we lived together as husband and wife. When we came back to New York, I told her the honeymoon is over. I would not abandon my two lovely children.

Of course it will occur to readers of this, my autobiography, that I was ready to abandon my children and stay forever in the Soviet Union when I thought everything would be rosy there. Yes. I admit that. But in that case I would have been helping to build the socialist dream, so I felt I could make such a sacrifice. Better to be honest here: If I stayed there, I would not have had to face my wife and children. But when I saw the misery in Brailov, I realized I had lived in America too long. I was spoiled. I had not the stamina to withstand the hardships of Soviet life. As for the girl, Ethel, maybe I didn't want to start with another woman, another family, more responsibilities. Yes, I was selfish and spoiled.

When we parted, Ethel cried. But she believed me when I said my duty comes first to my family. I didn't forget her for a long time.

Thirty-six years passed by. Life passed by. My hair turned white. My children brought forth a third generation, five lovely, decent grandchildren they gave me. Before I looked around I was an old man. Life had nothing more in store for me, right? Wrong.

One night I was sitting watching the news. The announcer was telling about Vietnam. I saw that the ground was covered with old people, women, and children, some dead, some on their knees begging for mercy from our boys. I broke down and cried. God, I cried, is there no justice in this world of ours? Why do we kill and murder poor people who have never done us any wrong? Just then the phone rang. Right away I recognized her voice. "Ethel! Where are you?" I said. She was visiting friends in my city.

My wife was alive, but we lived separate by then. Ethel came to my apartment. She was gray, but still an attractive woman. She had had an interesting life. She lived in Israel on a kibbutz and was married there, but divorced her husband because he had other women. After the war she went to Germany to help settle the concentration camp survivors. She married later, again, in Canada. When she came to see me her husband was still alive, but he was a sick man.

Ethel spent ten days with me. She would not allow me to touch her. She did not want to deceive her husband. "I respect him," she said, "even though I don't love him as I loved you. I wanted to see you once more, but my duty is to my sick husband."

She went back home to Canada, but life brought us together once more. When her husband died she came to live with me. Age was not an obstacle to our love. It took another form than in our younger days. It was something I have no word for. We walked, we talked, we could still touch each other. We agreed on everything. We had only one year together before she, too, died, but it was the happiest year of my entire life.

I have written down everything I can remember. My life began in a cold, dark room in old Russia. I knew great poverty and hunger there. I lived through wars and a great revolution. I was all my life on the side of the underprivileged, on the side of justice for the poor people that are under the heel of the richer classes. As a husband I wasn't ideal, but I tried to be a good father and grandfather. For a little while I had happiness in love. This is my autobiography. In the bottom drawer are copies for whoever wants one.

BEYOND THE PALE

—

You know what a pale is? Probably you do.
I had to look it up. A pale is a picket, as in
fence. All my life when I heard about the
Pale of Settlement I imagined snow falling
softly, perpetually, on Jewish villages, once
upon a time.

—

We lived in Washington Heights because
my father had a garage there. Daddy liked

us to live near where he worked so that he could run home when he forgot something; if business was slow, he could take a snooze. When that happened, he'd send my mother to watch the garage. It never occurred to me how strange this was. Driving is what the garage business is all about, and Mama didn't know how to drive. A customer comes, he leaves his car on the ramp to be parked; another customer comes, he waits for someone to retrieve his car from behind three other cars. Mama couldn't even pump gas. She'd sit reading in the office—a makeshift cubicle with a kerosene stove—and by and by a customer would show up. Then another. "Just a minute. Just a minute," Mama would say frantically. "The boss had an emergency. He'll be back soon."

"What's the emergency?" a customer once said to me.

"Oh, no emergency, he's just sleeping," I said.

Mama heard that and pulled me aside. "I'm not going to tell Daddy what you said."

—

When I was about seven years old, we moved to the corner of Edgecombe Avenue and 167th Street, which was a little closer to the garage. By this time we'd lived in four or five different apartments in the city, but this new one is the first I remember whole.

Our building was like the others on the street, a six-story

walk-up. We lived on the third floor. The apartment was more hall than rooms: You opened the front door into a long, long, windowless hallway, so narrow that even my little arms could touch the sides without straightening. At the very end of the hall was the bathroom; to the left of the bathroom, the kitchen, to the right, the living room. My mother and father slept in the living room. My room opened directly from theirs. Looking east, out my window, I could see the Harlem River and the Bronx beyond it, and on game nights, the sky blazed with lights from the Polo Grounds.

We lived on Edgecombe Avenue for about six years. Mornings at seven, while we ate breakfast, and evenings at six, while we had supper, the Second World War played on the kitchen radio.

"Daddy," I said. "What will they talk about on the radio when the war is over?"

"Don't worry about it," he said.

President Roosevelt died on Edgecombe Avenue. When Mama and I came home that afternoon, she went to the bathroom and I went to the kitchen and turned on the radio.

"Mama," I called, after I'd listened a minute. "They're saying that President Roosevelt died."

Through the closed door she called back, "No, darling. They're just talking about what would happen *if* he died."

She came into the kitchen and we listened together and began to cry.

It was funny about President Roosevelt. We loved him, but it seemed to me that I could remember a time when we didn't. Something about him being a "warmonger" and the war being "imperialist." Now, of course, all anybody talked about was Roosevelt and Stalin and Churchill, our Great Allied Leaders. This state of affairs had lasted so long that I was sure my memory was playing tricks. So I said I would give President Roosevelt my cat.

This is how that happened. I loved my cat, Cutie, more than anything, but it's true she was a nuisance, always running up and down the fire escape, crying to be let in or out, staying away all night, coming home with her ears torn. One day my father came home from the garage and I heard him say, in a low voice, to my mother, "Where's the kid?"

I was in my room. He came in, which he didn't often do, and sat down on my bed.

"You know what happened today?" This was going to be important.

"Faye Emerson came to the garage." I knew who Faye Emerson was; everybody did. She was the beautiful actress married to President Roosevelt's son Elliott.

"Faye Emerson said that President Roosevelt heard about Cutie and he wants to take her to live at Hyde Park."

President Roosevelt! Hyde Park! I could hardly believe it! Such honor! My Cutie, living with the Roosevelts on a big estate, playing with Fala! Of course she must go! There was the war effort to consider!

So one day, not long after she requested my cat, Faye Emerson (though probably she sent her chauffeur) came to get Cutie. That's what must have happened, because when I came home from school, Cutie was gone. Don't you think that's what happened?

—

Edgecombe Avenue was a hill, with the Polo Grounds at the bottom and us at the top. It was like a suburb of Harlem where richer Negroes lived. Our building was just an ordinary tenement, but there were apartment houses farther down Edgecombe that were palatial, with marble lobbies and elevators and doormen. Joe Louis lived on Edgecombe, but I never saw him.

On our actual block, which ran from Edgecombe to Amsterdam Avenue, there were only Italians. Italians sat on the stoops and spoke Italian, they called out the windows in Italian, they drank red wine from water glasses and ate Italian ices. Then, there was that September when we came back from Goldens Bridge to find that all those Italians had morphed into Negroes.

Three long blocks to the west of Edgecombe was Broadway. But before you got there, you had to cross Amsterdam Avenue, where the trolleys ran, and then St. Nicholas Avenue. Those streets, and the cross streets, were Spanish and Irish streets. Jews lived farther uptown on Broadway and along Fort Washington Avenue. Each block on the route to Broadway was a separate state, with borders to be negotiated.

Like the day I was walking west on 169th Street on my way to see my aunt Rachile and my cousin Vivian. They lived on 174th, just off Broadway. Suddenly I found myself surrounded by the Irish. (It's silly to say you can't tell what people are by looking at them; I knew they were Irish and, they, as you'll see in a minute, knew what I was.)

"What are you doing on this block?" the biggest kid said.

"I'm just going to Broadway."

"I bet you're a Jew," he said. And then the chorus, "Yeah, she's a *Jew!*" The circle tightened.

Every nerve in my body screamed *NO I'M NOT!*, but it was as plain as the nose on my face that no matter what I said, the die was cast. I might as well get something out of the beating. I took a deep breath. "Yeah," I said. "And what are you going to do about it!" As I tell it now, it was worth it.

———

When I was grown up, I met a guy named Jack (actual name), who'd gone to DeWitt Clinton High School with James Baldwin. Jack thought that this connection reflected well on him. He managed to mention it often, apropos or not: "Jimmy Baldwin said . . . When Jimmy Baldwin and I went . . ." And we, his friends, had the distinct feeling that should you say to Jack something on the order of "Hey, Jack, did you have any other Negro friends besides James Baldwin?", Jack would answer, "*Negro? I* never noticed he was *Negro!*"

Well, Mama was a little like Jack. If someone said to her, "So you live in a Negro neighborhood?" Mama would say, "We live in a neighborhood of working people."

Of course she was under orders. In those days no one (and by "no one" I mean we Communists) knew when he or she might be accused of White Chauvinism. Somebody would report you; you were brought up on charges before local leaders. You searched your memory: *What* did I *do?*

"*Didn't you ask Comrade Jones if he wanted his coffee black?*"

It was like those Irish kids who beat me up: Once the gang

formed, you might as well agree to the accusation, for all the good denial would do you.

———

So now I was getting older and junior high school loomed. Our address would funnel me directly into Stitt Junior High, two blocks away, on Edgecombe Avenue.

I said, "Mama, I don't want to go."

I was scared. I had *reason*. And, of course, the reason was unspeakable; in fact, neither Mama nor I mentioned the fact that ninety percent of the kids at Stitt were Negro. School was a dangerous place. You needed allies. And I already knew (and maybe Mama even remembered from her own school days among the Christians) that allies were more likely to come in your own color and creed.

Considering her choices—for daughter, against doctrine— Mama was brave. She took a chance that the comrades wouldn't notice, and in my last year of grade school she told school authorities that I was going to live with my aunt on 174th Street. From that address I would be poised for a more congenial junior high—that is, a school that was maybe forty percent Negro, the rest divided between Spanish, Jewish, Italian, Irish. Mike Lugo was Italian.

———

I'd been in love before. With Freddy Bloom, who left me waiting in front of the Coliseum Theatre on 181st Street on a cold spring day and broke my heart. With Richard Borrow, who was in my sixth grade class and liked another girl better. With Barry Axelrod, the park director, who wrote a play and made me his star. (I had such a bad case of stage fright that I peed in my pants onstage, in front of everyone, and was too ashamed to ever speak to him again.)

Mike Lugo was a rough, tough Catholic boy, beyond the Pale beyond any doubt. I was his girl; nobody messed with me when he was around. My association with him brought me a place in the world, and enough friends so that I was going to have a thirteenth birthday party.

—

We were on our way to Macy's to buy a dress for my party when I said to my mother, "Please, Mama. Do it the regular way."

I meant that just this once she shouldn't humiliate me. She and my aunts had a technique for buying clothes for special occasions. First, of course, you chose a dress. But a major consideration in making your choice was whether the tags were in a position to be easily tucked in, because, once worn for the occasion, the dress was to be returned. The transaction was filled with anxiety at every step. Would the tags dangle from the sleeve when worn? Would you get a stain on the dress? When returned, would the salesgirl notice that the dress had been worn?

"But, darling," Mama said. "When will you ever wear it again?"

"*Please*, Mama." So we bought a dress outright, a black taffeta number, princess-style, with a sweetheart neckline. My first black dress.

———

I don't remember very much about the party. I'm sure I was nervous. I have an image of a crowd in our so-called living room. I know that Sheila Minnick and Anna Hernandez and her brother Ray were there, and Diana Contafacilis too. I think my parents had agreed to stay in the kitchen and let us close the doors to the living room. But did we have music? Did we dance? What did we eat and drink?

All I remember (because, really, what is a party about if not about sex?) is that Mike Lugo and I went into my bedroom.

He closes the door. The lights are off and we're lying on my bed, kissing, crushing my black taffeta dress, and I'm thinking how lucky that it doesn't have to go back to Macy's. Mike is breathing urgently. He whispers something I can't quite hear.

What? I whisper back.

Can I touch your breast? he says.

Oh no, I say.

We kiss some more, and then he says, Promise me something.

What?

If you won't let me, promise you won't ever let anybody.

I promise, I say just as the door opens, and I see Mama framed in the light.

"Shame!" she cries.

—

Not long after that we moved from Edgecombe Avenue to Grand Street, on the Lower East Side. I think Mama was glad to get me out of Washington Heights. But it was a little late. I'd lived too long outside the Pale, associated too intimately with the Other, knew too well the advantages of such association. I knew altogether too much. I knew Cutie had gone to the pound, not Hyde Park. The cat was out of the bag, so to speak.

LILY'S BOND

—

My aunt Lily had not been lucky in love. First she fixed her heart on my father, and we've seen how that turned out. Next she set her sights on handsome Victor; he chose her youngest sister, Rachile. As far as I know she never fell for Norman, who was quite taken with Rachile, who in turn steered him to Frieda.

One way or another, all Lily's sisters were married when the Depression hit. At that time, as it happened, she was earning better than any of her sisters' husbands, and they had to borrow from her. That circumstance gave her some of her old cachet, as when, in the days before all those husbands, she'd pretty much run the family show.

In her work, at least, Lily had lucked into a good thing. She sold lingerie door-to-door. Now ask yourself: What kind of woman could afford, maybe even *need*, expensive silk and lace underwear in hard times? Right—Lily had a regular clientele of hookers. They were always in the market for something new, something more provocative, and they paid cash on the spot. I don't know how Lily got into this line of work, but when she fell in love again, in the early 1930s, she gave her route to my mother (to keep warm) and took off for California with a man named Tom. She hoped this would be *it*. Many years later I came across a photograph of the two of them with their arms around each other; somewhere in a sepia Midwest they leaned against Lily's great old car.

"Tell me!" I said to my mother. I'd never seen Lily looking so young and happy.

"It didn't work out," Mama said. "Lily had to take the train home. That was a good thing. She was a terrible driver."

Naturally Lily was dejected, but she retrieved her client list from my mother and went back to work. Not too much later she met Ben.

I like to think that they met through her work: she, arriving at a customer's apartment with her wares; he, on his way out, having paid a pretty penny to admire the wares on and off the model. One look at the redheaded saleslady and he loses his heart. Not likely. Probably it was a match made by a distant relative.

Lily was interested right away. Time was flying and Ben was plausible: the right age—middle thirties—no previous wives, tallish, with regular features, not at all bad-looking. What's more, unlike my father or my uncles Norman and Victor, those rough diamonds, Ben was a man of some refinement. He wrote poetry and played the violin. Lily was bringing culture to the family, and about time someone did! To earn a living—not much of a living, may it be said (and it was)—Ben gave music lessons.

He was a strange bird to land among these brothers-in-law. *Poetry! music!—he earns a living from this?* The brothers-in-law, often at odds among themselves, were united in suspicion. What is he, a sissy? my uncle Norman wondered. Maybe worse! my father suggested. And another thing: The man seemed to have no politics! Of course he was after Lily for her money; *that* they could understand. Well, just who did he think he was dealing with! Wasn't Lily's money a *family* resource?

Poor Ben. In the old country, he would have had respect. He would have been a scholar, a rabbi even, entitled to a wife who kept him while he spent all day at his books. And it wasn't fair to Lily to speak of her as if she had no attractions apart from her earnings. My father and Victor may have passed up their chance with her, but she was a nice-looking woman, even if no beauty like the other sisters. She knew how to take care of herself. She wore makeup, her wavy auburn hair was stylishly bobbed, and she was always fashionably dressed compared to her sisters, who claimed to despise bourgeois fashion and female artifice. ("As long as it's clean," Mama would say whenever I balked at a hand-me-down; my father's notion of a compliment was "It's neat," meaning exactly that.)

Of course Lily did have some drawbacks. She had inherited a family tendency to bronchitis; as for personality, let's say that she was something of a scold. "You look like a greenhorn, Belle," she nagged at my mother, until Mama cut off the black braids that had adorned her like a coronet and got a horrible perm instead.

The worst thing Lily did for my mother's good was to

burn all her papers. That was during the McCarthy years: Mama's compositions, essays, letters—all up in smoke. Poor Mama. Those papers meant the world to her; they were her real American citizenship papers. She had earned them in hard-won months at Brookwood Labor College, at Bryn Mawr Summer School for Working Women, at Barnard Summer School where, always, she was the favorite of her teachers, praised for her intelligence and her writing. (But that's another story.) She never forgave Lily.

To get back to Ben. His brothers-in-law may have been a little crude in their judgment, but there *was* something creepy about my uncle Ben. Something unpleasant about his pale, slick skin, something Uriah Heepish in his elaborate deference. Now that I think of it, I wonder if his unfortunate snuffle was his way of showing that he was looking down his nose at us: With closed mouth, he would push air through his nose with a sound something like a flooded engine—if you liked him you could assume he was clearing his nasal passages; if not, you could take it as his opinion of you.

In my mother, though, Ben sensed a sympathetic soul. She admired music (in theory only; in real life she was tone-deaf), she valued education, and she revered the printed word. Ben took to writing her long letters.

Dear Bella,

With the winter months to be here soon, you will proba-
bly need reading matter to while away the howling win-
ter nights. Here are a few pages that might help you out.
There are plenty of people reading my scribbling, so you'll
merely join the flock. I hope your response won't be too
unfavorable . . .

You see the problem. Those mixed messages—the desperate plea for understanding, the defensive offensiveness, the
readiness with which he was prepared to take umbrage.
What a sensitive plant he was! Who could assuage him?
When one of Ben's thick envelopes arrived, my mother
sighed deeply: Once again a wrong had been done him. But
she always read the letter, and she always answered. Not to
answer would only add another wrong, which would duly appear in his next letter.

———

For many years Lily and Ben lived in the Highbridge section
of the Bronx. Two little rooms for just the two of them. They
had no children. Lily worked as a saleslady, Ben gave a few violin lessons. They weren't spenders. Lily kept a lot of her
money in a joint account with my mother. And, as you'll see,
she had a savings bond destined for Frieda. For Ben, he had a

roof over his head and his meals. Sometimes I imagined the sounds that filled the little apartment when they were alone: Ben's flooded-engine snuffle, Lily's bronchial cough.

There came a time, some twenty years into the marriage, when Lily's bronchitis worsened. She coughed up blood. Her doctor urged a change of climate. She went to Florida. After a week, she wrote to Ben: "Very, very good, Ben. This air does something to me. It's hot, but it's soothing. People love it here. I love it." A week later she wrote again: "I think I'll stay longer, Ben. I feel good here." And two weeks later: "I want to stay here. I am not coming back to New York. This is the place where I have to live."

Ben was beside himself. What was the meaning of this? Was Lily leaving him? Did she mean for him to join her? Myself, I think she meant to get rid of him but lost her nerve. Because in answer to his panicked letter, she wrote: "It's up to you, Ben. Think it over and think hard. Answer me."

I remember [he wrote to Mama] *standing, looking around me in our little apartment, the small living room with the little kitchen behind the screen, the few chairs, the couch where Lily and I sat—how long?—many years, living our life here, confronting our problems, planning our days. In the bedroom the bookcase near the bed, all so familiar, and all to be gone, never to be seen again. Limbs one is born with, and other parts one annexes through life, and all become part of one, and one retains some and must sever himself from the others. And a strange organ, the heart, too, immediately involved in all of this. It can flutter with no weight at all, or be loaded down with a ponderous burden. Can gush streams of joy, or discharge a deluge of unhappiness, and can dispense what flavor one desires—bitter or sweet. That day I recall a dribble of fear steal into my body. A premonition? Uncertainty became my companion.*

You can see the man had feeling for the written word, but, oh, the pathos! He was in his fifties by then, with no financial hopes except for the living he eked out with music lessons; with no stomach for life on his own. He faced the truth: He was lost without Lily. She held all the cards—and not only the money. He answered her letter posthaste, forgetting even to assume an attitude. "If Florida is the place for you to live, then it will be my place too. Let me know what to do. How to go about joining you. Because I really don't know how to begin." It was almost a love letter.

So the marriage continued by default. Lily sent detailed instructions about how he was to pack up the apartment. And then she gave him a final task. "Remember the package we keep in Norman's safe," she wrote. "The bond is in it, and also the key to our safety deposit box. Don't get these things until the day before you leave so you will be sure not to lose them. They are everything we have in the world."

Ben had lots of time to contemplate the future as he dismantled the small apartment. The problem was, could he ever reassemble *himself?* He knew no one in Florida, only a cousin and the woman's husband. What was his name? Sam! So shifty-eyed, such a monstrous braggart! He was giving up *everything* by joining Lily, burning all his rickety bridges to life. He burned with resentment too. Well, no point thinking about it, he had no choice.

There wasn't much time left. It was already Wednesday. On Thursday he would have to wait in the apartment for the movers; on Friday morning his train was leaving. It was time to get the package and the key from Norman, retrieve the valuables from the bank, and say good-bye to the family. Suddenly he had tender feelings for the family. He imagined friendly handshakes and good wishes, promises to visit soon. *I'll feel a lot better when I see them, I surely will.*

———

In those days, Norman had a garage. So did my father. In fact, they had once been partners in the garage business. Two pigheaded men in business together? Two pigheaded men, each determined to prevail? Please! Their wives told them that it was a terrible idea, but, being pigheaded, they paid no attention. They split up in less than a year, and then they had to sort out the complications of a partnership gone bad; my father went around bad-mouthing Norman. Naturally, that got back to Frieda, who stormed into our apartment one day and, in front of my mother, let my father have it. He took it sitting down. God, I wish I'd seen that.

Anyway, on the Wednesday before his Friday departure, Ben went off to see Norman. He was uneasy about the errand. Just why, he couldn't have said. He was already at the subway when he rushed back to the apartment to get Lily's letter. That was a clue.

At Norman's garage, Ben feigned nonchalance.

I spoke casually, telling him of our decision to move to Florida, saying I came for the package we had in his safe, since the key to our bank box was there, and also, I said, the bond in which Lily had made Frieda the beneficiary. Lily wanted to have everything, since she didn't know what she may need. I commented on what a job it was making the move and the work it involved.

Busy as I was talking, I didn't notice the peculiar expression on Norman's face. When I did look up, he had his eyes squinting as he peered at me suspiciously, while a frown

covered his face. "I don't know. I don't know," he mumbled.
Next moment he got up and began pacing back and forth in
front of his desk, his eyebrows lowered, his eyes trying to
penetrate through me. For a moment it occurred to me that
perhaps he didn't have the key to the safe.

"I have it! I have it!" he answered.

I couldn't believe it! He hesitated to give me the pack-
age! I hastily took Lily's letter from my pocket and placed
it on the desk.

"Here is Lily's letter," I said irritably.

"She didn't write me nothing," he complained. ["Not-
ting" is actually how Ben rendered the word.] *He stood there*
obstinately. He didn't even reach for the letter. Did he con-
sider it a forgery?

He became more conciliatory. He sat down. "You see,
Ben," he said. "I'm Lily's guardian. I have to protect her.
Come back tomorrow and we'll see."

I looked at him. So. My wife had a guardian! I
didn't know that. I wonder what would happen, Bella, if
some man told Rosen that he was your *guardian? Rosen*
would probably give you away to him altogether.

Norman suspected him of trying to steal his own wife's
property! Was he worried about the bond, the bond that
would go to Frieda? My God, he'd like to punch Norman in

the nose! But there was no time. Tomorrow the movers were coming, he wouldn't be able to go back to Norman's. How could he go to Florida without the package? Ah! Bella would help him.

You and Rosen were in the kitchen when I arrived. When Rosen saw me his expression was as if something unsavory had met his eyes. My experience with Norman sort of clipped my wings. It stuck in my throat and I couldn't say anything about it. In a subdued voice I explained that I needed someone to come to my apartment tomorrow when the movers will come. Would Bella please come?

Well, Rosen immediately objected. Bella has to go to Goldens Bridge, Bella has no time. I tried to plead my case, but Rosen was adamant. And, you, Bella, were silent. But then you turned to me and looked in my face. You said you will be in my apartment tomorrow morning. The heaviness in my heart lifted.

Rosen was angry. When I said good-bye he turned away and did not answer. Surely it was the first time in recorded history that a man did not offer a handshake and good wishes to a brother-in-law going off to a new life.

The next day Ben once again took the subway to Norman's. When he got there, Norman was shooting the breeze with a couple of men. Norman noticed Ben's arrival. He continued his conversation. Ben waited. Five minutes. Ten minutes. The worm turned. *I want that package! Give me that package!*

All right, all right, said Norman. Here!

Is everything in there?

Yes, yes.

But everything wasn't. The bond, which Frieda was to inherit at Lily's death, was missing. This strange bird of a brother-in-law wasn't to be trusted. (Of course the whole thing was moot anyway; Lily outlived Frieda by many years.)

———

In Miami, Ben told Lily what had happened.

"Forget about it," Lily said. "Norman didn't mean anything."

Ben wrote to Bella and told her everything.

"Norman didn't mean anything," Bella wrote back.

Family waters closed over the incident.

———

Lily and Ben lived in Miami for the rest of their lives. They ran a boardinghouse, two long bus rides from the beach. Once every few years, in summertime—because that's when the boardinghouse had empty rooms—my parents would make the drive down. I know that Norman and Frieda went down to visit, too. Everyone behaved very well. Nothing was ever mentioned about the little trouble with the package. Every other year or so, Lily would come by herself to New York.

It was quite astonishing that Lily, whose health had always been precarious, lived for such a long time. She and Ben got old in Miami. They sold the boardinghouse and bought a little two-room apartment. When she was well up in her eighties, Lily said to my mother, "My traveling days are over," and soon my mother's traveling days were over, too; she and Lily kept in touch mostly by mail. Now and then Ben would write to my mother, rehearsing old grievances.

One day we heard from my uncle Joe, who also lived in Miami. Lily and Ben were not doing well. Lily couldn't go outside without a walker, and Ben wouldn't let her use the walker outside; he was ashamed of this infirm old lady. And Lily was becoming senile. She couldn't shop or cook; there was almost no food in the house except what Ben brought. Joe described a raw chicken rotting in the refrigerator.

Well, we got busy. We got in touch with social workers; we made a large donation to a decent nursing home and got them moved in. They lived there for a number of years.

As Lily declined, Ben flourished. The nursing home was a great venue for him. He gave readings of his poetry, he read his stories, edited a little newsletter, organized concerts. He was at last a man of consequence.

I took my mother down to see Lily twice during her last years. A week after our second visit, Lily died. We said she had been waiting to see Mama one last time.

And here's something that won't surprise you. To this day I don't know whether Ben is dead or alive. The minute Lily died, we dropped him like a hot potato.

AN AMERICAN GIRL

—

In our family no one (by which I mean my mother and my aunts) was chatty on the telephone. Telephones were for terse, urgent messages: Meet me at Macy's. . . . The kid is sick. . . . The meeting is postponed. . . . My mother would even run the few blocks to the garage rather than phone my father there. In fact, it seems to me that we didn't even *have* a phone in the house until I was about twelve.

This habit of not telephoning at the drop of a hat was meant to save money; and in my family this was not only a virtue but a cause: *We are not spoiled Americans who gossip all day. We know the value of a dollar.* And, it could be added, *Don't forget the starving people of China.*

Another benefit of the sparing use of the telephone was that we got lots of mail. Anyone with information to pass along wrote, even from Brooklyn to the Bronx. *So* many letters. There was hardly a day when my mother didn't get a letter from her cousin Sylvia or my aunt Lily. Hundreds of letters. I found some of them squirreled around the house after my mother died. But although I looked particularly, I could not find even one letter from my aunt Sally. What *wouldn't* I give to read Aunt Sally's letters again!

Sally was my uncle Oscar's second wife. "An American girl" was how my mother and her sisters referred to her. This was not simply descriptive of the fact that Sally had been born in Brooklyn; no. It meant: American girls are *spoiled* girls, spoiled by America. They think they have *everything* coming to them.

How do I know this is what they meant? Because when it was what they meant, they called *me* an American girl.

(And speaking of second wives, we had another one in our family. My uncle Joe had a second wife, but he was irreproachably a widower when he came by her. Uncle Oscar was divorced.)

—

Oscar was the firstborn son—traditionally, the hope of the family. He was the eldest brother, the gentlest of uncles. Other uncles played rough and teased. Uncle Oscar took me in his lap and crooned "Brown Eyes" (in Russian). But to tell the truth, Oscar was a little . . . how to put it? Slow? Passive? Timid? Some people called him simple, meaning retarded, but that wasn't so. Oscar found the world perplexing; and, as his sisters seemed to understand everything, he put himself in their hands.

Oscar's first wife was Beatrice. Of Beatrice herself I have no memory but an old wedding photo: Oscar dressed in top hat and tails yearning over his bride; Beatrice, despite full wedding regalia, seems quite businesslike. I think Beatrice was a distant family connection from Canada, and I've heard that she was a formidably strong-minded girl. The sisters, being strong-minded girls themselves, probably thought she was just what Oscar needed. As for Beatrice, I don't know what she thought she was getting into, but I don't think she had many notions of love.

To say the marriage was not a success is to say that Mount Everest is a bump in the road. More and more frequently, as time passed, Oscar appeared at the door of one or another of his sisters to complain that Beatrice was treating him badly; close on his heels, Beatrice appeared, complaining to her sisters-in-law that their brother was a simpleton and good-for-nothing as a husband.

The sisters conferred many times on this subject. They could not bear to see Oscar so unhappy, and eventually they decided there was nothing for it but that the marriage should end. There were a few details to be worked out: the child (yes, there was a child), the store (Oscar and Beatrice ran a delicatessen), alimony.

Alimony? Who ever heard of alimony? What is this Beatrice—an American girl? We've said she can keep the store and the child! Does she think we'll let the child *starve?*

"No alimony," said the sisters to Oscar.

This piece of advice landed Oscar in alimony jail.

"Look," my father would say when we passed Bronx debtors' prison on our drive upstate. "Uncle Oscar's college!"

Beatrice was bitter about the sisters, particularly about my mother, whom she saw, no doubt correctly, as the ringleader in the plot against her. She cut off all connection with the family. Oscar moved in with my aunt Frieda. A few years later, a matchmaker introduced him to Sally.

—

Sally. I'd never seen the like of her. Sally was square and close to the ground. Her unbelievably black hair was piled into a pompadour in front; a black net caught the fall at her shoulders. She wore bright red lipstick and rouge to match. She was lively and pure Brooklyn. You might think that Oscar would prefer the deliberately unadorned style of his sisters, but, no, he liked Sally. After their first date, he asked his sisters if he should pop the question.

"Take your pajamas!" my grandfather called as Oscar left the house for his second date.

—

Sally had never been married, and, not being a spring chicken, she had had plenty of time to look around and codify her ideas about the proper way to approach marriage. First came the engagement. The engagement, as everyone who wasn't a greenhorn knew, was announced with a ring. Not a sweet garnet in an antique setting, not a few diamond chips cunningly set, not even your simple but elegant quarter-carat solitaire. A *full* carat of diamond surrounded by appropriately sized baguettes.

This was a real jaw-dropper for the sisters. A diamond engagement ring! Who did Sally think she was? Who did she think *Oscar* was? Who did she think *they* were? You only had to glance at their hands to know what they would think about diamond rings: eight working hands, rough and thickened at the knuckle, bare of polish, innocent of any jewel, including even gold wedding bands. Who ever heard of a diamond engagement ring in this family? It costs *how much?*

But Oscar wanted to get married. And Frieda, who had her hands full not only with her own family but with my grandmother, who was also living with her, *and* Oscar, all of them in a small house in Jackson Heights, *really* wanted Oscar married.

"Let her have the ring," Frieda said.

Lily was scornful. "*Believe* me. She'll take him without a ring." My aunt Rachile was against the ring, probably because my mother was for it; Mama was for it, for Frieda's sake; and that, together with Oscar's plea, tipped the balance. I was thrilled. I couldn't wait to see this ring. I was certainly going to have one when my time came. Didn't they call me an American girl?

———

Whether from Brooklyn, where they first lived, or later, from Miami, Sally kept in close touch with her sisters-in-law. She was a brilliant correspondent: Nothing came between her and the immediate moment. She wrote as she spoke, a mile a minute, untroubled by the rules of punctuation or an internal censor. And like all great writers, she had her subject—in this case, the social activities of her family, and how much they cost.

Bessie married off her daughter Sandra last Sunday it was a grand affair, Sandra's dress was white satin with seed pearls on the bodice and Bessie told me it cost $132.65 wholesale if they had bought retail it would have been $322.98. She didn't have a train which was really a shame because it would have been another $40 but Bessie said Sandra might anyway want to dye the dress and wear it on another occasion and then they would have to cut the train off so it wasn't worth it. I have to say that Sandra looked very nice even so. Before the ceremony they had appetizers a very nice spread with whitefish, and Nova, they paid $3.95 a person, after the ceremony we sat down to a regular dinner, with roast beef or chicken, seltzer and sodas, schnapps, all you wanted $5.95 a person. Sandra's going away suit was pale blue, which she wore with matching shoes, very nice, $35 but I think beige would have been better. I wore my green silk, which I paid for $48.50 in Klein's which it's worth it because I get a lot of wear from it. Oscar wanted to

wear his brown suit but I told him blue was better and for
once he listened and we bought him a blue suit very dark
$60 but he'll have it for a long time and if he ever needs a
black suit he can wear it instead.

This is a reconstitution from memory, a shadow of the real thing. Sally's letters were treasured in our family, read aloud, sent to relatives in distant places, with instructions to be sent on to other relatives. Oh, how we laughed as my mother read them! The four sisters, sitting around the kitchen table, laughing and laughing; Mama laughing so hard she couldn't get the words out. I'd say Sally gave good value.

———

In due time, Sally and Oscar retired to Miami.

"Retired from *what?*" my father wanted to know.

They lived out their final years in a single room in one of those little run-down hotels on the Beach, in company with other old people who'd managed to save a few dollars. Early-bird specials, doggie bags, cronies on the beach, organized activities—it was, I think, a pleasant life. My uncle Joe moved to Miami Beach, and my aunt Lily lived a bus ride away. Oscar looked very natty when we saw him, dressed by Sally in a straw hat, a nice clean shirt, and plaid pants that belted above his belly. Sally's hair remained as unbelievably black as ever, her lips and cheeks as brightly red. She took up folk dancing, for which she had a wardrobe of peasant blouses with alarming décolletage. How her diamond ring sparkled as she do-si-doed!

—

A few years ago I pinned a cartoon to my bulletin board: A man and a woman are driving through the countryside. They approach a road marker that reads FEAR NO EVIL. The woman says, "*We made good time. We're already in the valley of the shadow of death.*"

Those old people, my family, my uncle Oscar and aunt Sally, my uncle Joe, my aunt Lily and her husband Ben— they weren't going to be able to hold on much longer. Of course they had one foot in the grave, but they were also in trouble, demographically speaking.

Have you been to Miami Beach recently? Just as my old folks were dying off, their havens were being discovered. Who could have guessed that their seedy little hotels were Art Deco treasures? A little renovation here and there, a neon sign, some pink and turquoise paint; they turned out to be just the ticket for a lifestyle. If *Sally* was an American girl, who were *these* people?

But you know what I still wonder about? Who got Sally's ring?

LIKE GODS

—

We read the letters of the dead like
*   helpless gods,*
yet gods for all that, since we know
*   the dates to come . . .*

—Wisława Szymborska

February 25, 1958

Dear Miss Thornbury:

   Your assignment asking your students to
tell you "Why am I taking up typing?" appears to be a simple one. The answer is not

simple. It becomes even more difficult to write about it when one remembers your remark that we needn't tell anything of a personal nature. The reasons which prompted me at this time to try to learn typing is personal and complex.

It is true that since my daughter's marriage we have to chase after her every time my husband needs to do some typing. But it would be telling only some of the truth if I was to stop right here: the need for typing in my husband's business amounts to a couple of letters a year. Besides, our daughter lives in our vicinity and has been willing to type these letters for her father.

Once or twice in the past, I toyed with the idea of trying my hand at a typewriter, but there was always a fear that I will never learn. There has always been talk about high school kids who learn quickly, and acquire speed in no time. So I used to take refuge in the belief that there are more important things to do—leaving typing to the young.

Last May—to be exact, on the 23rd—something occurred which shook my world to its very depth. A sister of mine with whom I enjoyed an unusually good relationship, was hit by an out-of-control automobile while waiting with another friend for me to keep a luncheon appointment. Her life came to an end that day; my life became some-what distorted: it felt as though the bottom had dropped out of my world. One resolution after another to become realistic about the situation would depart in great haste—leaving me in great distress.

"Develop new relationships, develop new interests," wise friends were advising me in those trying days, which were long and many. As weeks turned into months, I gradually began to realize that I was doing my sister no good by indulging in self-pity, so I began to explore possibilities of busying myself in the hope that little time would remain for brooding and reciting the events of that fateful afternoon again and again.

When Personal Typing given at the "Y" in the afternoons, came to my attention, I felt that this course would meet my needs. Little did I suspect then—two months ago—that I would find the work fascinating and even intriguing. It presented a challenge to me. At first I was frightened and was inclined more than once to drop the course. But this is where you, Miss Thornbury, come in! Always, some-how at a psychological moment, I would hear you saying: "Class, don't aim at a perfect paper," . . . or that very timely encouraging remark "Class, don't get discouraged."

I have also been admiring your resourcefulness at being able to teach a large class and find time for individual instruction. In short, with your aid, I learned that typing is a many-folded skill. It means not only learning the *keyboard*, but various techniques of the machine; one also improves his vocabulary, spelling and the division of words.

In my case typing proved to be therapy in the sense that I gained time to make if not peace, then some kind of a truce with a situation which is irrevocable and therefore not solvable. Last but surely not least, I fear no more "those high school kids." They constitute no threat to my security any longer. At times I feel as "accomplished" as Eliza Doolittle from *My Fair Lady*. She did it—and so did I!

Gratefully,

B. Rosen

November 17, 1998

Dear Ms. Thornbury,

I came across the above letter a few months ago and have been wondering what you thought when you read it. Did you realize at once that it was the work of the quiet, sixty-ish woman who sat in the last row of your class? You checked the typing for accuracy, of course; I see that there were a few mistakes, but on the whole I'd say your pupil reflects credit on you. What about grammar? Surely you noted that the syntax was not that of a native English speaker; but the writer had mastered English pretty well, don't you think? And the style? Full marks for eloquence! And I can assure you that the flattery was sincere. But, Ms. Thornbury, *what* did you think when you suddenly came upon that *cri de coeur?*

I am, of course, the daughter referred to in paragraph two and I did, indeed, do my father's bits of typing: "Dear Mr. Brown; your bill is two months past due. This state of affairs cannot continue . . ."

I imagine, Ms. Thornbury, that you were a woman of some sensibility, perhaps a retired teacher of English still wishing to be active. Your evident education and refinement inspired my mother to make you her confidante. Or it may simply be that, with her fingers placed correctly on the keyboard, she could not help pressing those keys that expressed her heart. Whatever the case, I would like to do as my mother did and take you into my confidence.

As my mother mentioned, I was married the year before she entered your class. My marriage lasted only two years and some months longer; those years seemed like a dream to me then, and so they do now.

But such odd things stay in the mind. For instance, my new mother-in-law asked me to call her Mother White.

She was a Christian Scientist. She looked just like Spring Byington. I can see her now in her dainty frocks chirping about "error." I mean no disrespect to Christians, Ms. Thornbury, but they do let it be known that it's better to give, etc. Mother White (*never* did I bring myself to utter those words) invited me to her basement to see all the furniture she had no use for; really great stuff. Oh, I said, what a pretty bureau! And that dry sink! Sofas and wing chairs— she had everything. And weren't her son and I about to set up housekeeping? So *why* did she bring me down there if she wasn't going to offer us a single blessed stick of furniture? And *why*, with all that has followed, to say nothing of all the furniture that has passed through my life, is that something that still gets my goat?

Another thing is that my mother and I went shopping for my wedding dress. She, believing that a girl only gets married once, agreed to bypass Macy's and S. Klein on the Square and head straight to Fifth Avenue. We made the round of Saks, Lord & Taylor, and Bergdorf's. (She grew timid in the presence of an elegant saleswoman.) At De Pinna's (gone for many years) we found a pale gray taffeta dress, ballerina-length, with leg-o'-mutton sleeves and a scooped neckline. We went for it, despite the seventy-five-dollar price tag. We also ordered shoes dyed to match.

My uncle Georgie, who was a caterer, supplied the food for our wedding supper.

"You want two tiers or three?" he asked me about the cake.

"Two," I answered.

Georgie said to my mother, "We'll give her three."

And here, Ms. Thornbury, let me tell you something I never told my mother. On the very night of my wedding—it was a February night, during a winter thaw—I dreamed I was trying to remove my ring (intertwined strands of three colors of gold, bought in a shop called Wedding Rings, Inc., on Eighth Street). I pulled at the ring until my finger was red and swollen. It wouldn't come off.

In the morning (we honeymooned in Jamaica) depression took hold of me. I told myself it was only delayed wedding jitters. After all, for three years I had been desperately in love with this man. I'd chased him, I'd spied on him, I'd waited in the dark outside his house to see him bring home other girls. Finally I'd landed him.

When we met, I was not much more than eighteen, he was ten years older, a man of the world. For three years he led me, as they say, a merry dance. I lost my innocence with him. Not sexual innocence, Ms. Thornbury—young as I was, I had already lost that—but worldly innocence.

You, of course, know nothing of our family history, Ms. Thornbury, but you may take it as given that although I longed for frivolity (never even having heard the word), my worldview in no way allowed for lightness of character: "Not a serious person," is what my mother would have said of someone like me. I was given to understand that the world was a deadly serious place: The forces of history ran the show; class was arraigned against class for the final conflict, the light of the future against the dark of reaction. Some years earlier I had taken a step away from our peculiar family orthodoxy. And now, casually, as if it were a simple elaboration of my life, I stepped further, and gaily, with a stranger, into taxis and French restaurants, into theaters and even nightclubs, into a sailboat! You can imagine the effect on a girl like me, a girl of two minds. We both paid for that, my husband and I, but he paid more.

So now we come to the pivotal moment, Ms. Thornbury, the one that brought my mother to your class in Personal Typing. On May 23, 1957, she called me. It was late in the morning, maybe eleven or so. My mother didn't call very often. She didn't like to "intrude," as she often said. But should I let a week go by without calling her, she would take her courage in her hands.

"Darling," she said. "I'll be in the neighborhood later. Are you going to be home?"

I was always home. I didn't make the bed until around noon. After that maybe I'd get dressed—maybe. The hours somehow passed, one by one, until, thank God, it was time to cook dinner.

"I baked a chicken," my mother said. "You know Daddy doesn't like chicken."

She had to have an offering. Just to see me. Oh, if I could, I would go down on my knees to her . . . !

Then she said, "I have to go now. I'm late. I'm meeting Frieda and Rose for lunch."

Frieda and Rose. What was the *matter* with those women, standing *outside* the restaurant waiting for my mother? I'd learned *something* from my new life. I could have told them: Ladies go *into* the restaurant. They allow the waiter to seat them—they even order a drink as they wait for their companions. But no! Like greenhorns, Frieda and Rose stood in front of the plate-glass window, looking up and down the street for my mother, until the car smashed into them. And she, when she got there, and for years and years, and maybe until the moment of her death, *knew* it was her fault.

I was dressed at two o'clock when my cousin Sylvia called. "There's been an accident," she said.

"*Mama!*" I said.

"No, no. Frieda."

Until I came across my mother's letter to you, I had no idea of your existence in her life, Ms. Thornbury. I would like to report to you that for a number of years, my mother continued to use the skills you taught her. Practice did not much improve her; she was never a very good typist, but she was so proud of being able to do the thing at all. And, as you will have gathered, my husband and I divorced, with great bitterness on his side, and on mine a mixture of relief and fear. These days I often think of him with regret.

In time, my mother's typewriter broke down beyond repair. She never got a new one, and I resumed typing my father's correspondence: "Dear Mr. Smith, I have been very patient but your rent is now three months overdue. If this state of affairs continues I will be forced to take steps. . . ." After 1992, there was no further need for such typing.

GOOD-FOR-NOTHING

—

In June, at the end of my sophomore year, I dropped out of Hunter College.

"Why, darling? Tell me why," my mother said to me.

"What did you expect?" my father said to her.

He was right; she should have known she hadn't raised a scholar. All varieties of mathematics sent me into a tailspin. My ear for foreign languages was as bad as my ear for music. I had some hopes for biology until they handed me a frog and a scalpel. And those papers my English teacher had liked so much? They'd been written by my ex-boyfriend—ex-fiancé, actually.

Oh yes, I was seventeen and already I had a broken engagement on my record. That accounted for some of the bitterness behind Daddy's *What did you expect?* The question had wide application in the realm of projects undertaken and abandoned. Like dancing lessons. Like design school. Like an engagement, a quite promising engagement, to a law school graduate, complete with a ring (small pearl, *pace* Aunt Sally), a party, the meeting of prospective in-laws. And then—boom! All over. He saw what he was getting: a sullen, never-satisfied-no-matter-what-he-did baby brat. But he'd already written some of my English papers.

"Go ahead, see what it's like to earn a living," Daddy said. He was struck by another thought: "Who'd hire a good-for-nothing like you, anyway?"

That summer, the summer I was eighteen, I got a job at an insurance company on William Street. Of course I got it under false pretenses.

Insurance. On the first floor of the vast enterprise that was the Continental Casualty Company there were no offices, only desks. Gray metal desk after desk after desk; a battalion of desks, each manned by a policy writer or an underwriter.

You may think that "policy writer" is simply another name for "underwriter." That shows how little you know. The telling difference, in those days, was that the underwriters were guys and the policy writers were girls. The underwriters were the bosses of the policy writers. They spent most of their time on the phone selling policies: The underwriter got to lean way back in his chair, he could put his feet on the desk, he told jokes to his customers, he laughed and snickered.

When his work was done, the underwriter got up from his desk and walked over to a policy writer. He told her which policy he had just sold. The policy writer then plucked the appropriate policy form from stacks of such forms on her desk. You've seen this kind of document: dozens and dozens of paragraphs of boilerplate broken by blank spaces. The job of the policy writer was to fill in the blank spaces.

All day, from nine to five, I sat hunched miserably over my typewriter, clicking the roller past line after line of boilerplate, trying to adjust the spacing carefully when I reached the blank spaces, *hoping* I could fit the provision into the space, *praying* not to make a mistake, because if I did, I'd have to take a new form and start all over again. Oh, and did I mention the three carbon copies that had to be made? Most of the girls were pros; their wastebaskets were empty. *My* wastebasket was filled to overflowing with ruined forms, which, when no one was looking, I'd stuff in my bag to sneak out to the ladies' room to throw away. Everyone knew my days were numbered.

So this was what it was like to earn a living. As soon as I sat down at my desk in the morning, I'd start looking at the clock. I thought it was like being in hell. On the other hand, if the Catholic God was the true God, it must have been like being in heaven.

Insurance business was Catholic business, at least on this low rung: Sullivans, O'Learys, Albaneses, Marinos. The guys were Irish; the girls, Italian—or so I remember it. The girls lived on Staten Island and in Brooklyn; the guys lived in Washington Heights and the Bronx.

All the girls were engaged or about to be engaged. We girls were always going to lunch to celebrate someone's engagement. During the two ten-minute morning breaks, girls would gather in the ladies' room to show off engagement rings. Photos of fiancés were produced and admired. Serious discussions of wedding dresses and bridesmaids' dresses took place; likewise of living room sets and bedroom drapes. The approaching wedding was the focus of all attention, the future so settled that mention of it was hardly necessary. Nothing troubled my colleagues except a few intriguing questions: premarital sex ("If I really loved him . . .") and contraception . . . whether? (most said never!) in what circumstances? what kind?

After her wedding, a girl would live in the neighborhood where she had grown up, near her parents and aunts and uncles and cousins. She would go on working for a few months or a year, until the first baby came, and then there would be more babies. These girls were so happy. Happy in this moment of freedom from domestic responsibility, working and saving money for the future; happy that they had secured the future; happy in the approval of their families; very busily happy in planning for the ultimate event. I'd never seen such pure, unclouded happiness. I knew it wasn't for me, but I was envious.

And I *liked* being included in the talk about dresses and furniture and sex. I liked office conviviality, the teasing, the gossip, the flirting (engaged or not, there was a lot of policy writer–underwriter flirting). I myself flirted with a guy named Jerry Sullivan. He happened not to be married. (Most of the guys were.) We never actually went on a date, Jerry and I; the guys always went out in a group, but we necked in dark corners.

And who did they think *I* was, to let me in on all this? Because even though I thought I'd fooled them, they knew I was from another planet.

I told you I'd taken the job under false pretenses. It was just a little thing I did, hardly anything at all. I'd stopped thinking about it even; in fact you could say I'd forgotten that on my job application I'd moved the third letter of my last name four spaces to the alphabetic right. Until the day Jerry Sullivan said to me, "You've got a call on my line. It's your mother."

The full implications of this hit me at once. I almost fainted. I'd *told* my mother that she couldn't reach me, I'd *told* her I had no phone on my desk. Yet here she was; she'd tracked me down. She *knew!*

"Are you sure it's for me?" I asked Jerry.

"Oh yeah, it's for you. She asked for Dorothy Rowen."

Jerry Sullivan smiled.

—

A few years later I was married, with a new name, a new life. While my mother took typing lessons to ease her grief, I went skiing and sailing. I went dining and drinking with my husband and our friends. I was very depressed. How perverse! Then I got pregnant.

But why *not* have a baby? Bob, that was my husband's name, wanted a baby. And what else was I going to do? I had no education, no skills, no concrete ambitions, only insis-

tent, inchoate longings, and the above-mentioned depression. I'd wake up one morning and think: Okay, I'll have a
baby, that will settle everything. The next morning: No, if I
have a baby, nothing else will *ever* happen. On a day when I
thought I would, we told my parents.

Oh, they were thrilled! My father said, "Dots, you want a
house?" He was going to buy us a brownstone in the Village!
Something about that decided me. No. No baby. Think it
was spite?

Bob wasn't happy, but he said it was up to me. It was ille-
gal, of course, but I had the name of a doctor, a good doctor,
a European doctor, very skilled, very gentle. In those days
these doctors were precious gold, their names whispered
from ear to ear, written down on small pieces of paper, carried in the secret compartments of wallets. Skilled as they
were, the best of these doctors hurt you. They couldn't use
anesthetics, because you had to be able to walk out of the office pretty soon afterwards, and you were warned not to
scream. The next day I stayed in bed and called my parents.
Miscarriage, I said.

"Oh, darling, don't worry," my mother said. "You know,
I had a miscarriage, but afterwards I had you."

—

For months after that I dreamed about babies. Dreams are
boring, I know. I always skip them in books. But I'm going

to tell you this one because I haven't forgotten it in all these years.

A very dark night. I'm walking alone on a narrow street walled by tall buildings. Not a light shows anywhere. It's like being in a canyon, or maybe the financial district. Then, at the very top of a building, I see a lighted window. I enter the building and start climbing the stairs. I climb many flights until I come to the top floor. I open a door. In a bare room lit by a single unshaded bulb is Camille, a girl I recognize from the insurance company. She's holding a baby. It has red hair, like my husband's hair. As I stand there, the baby falls from her arms and hits its head on the floor. It's dead. I'm horrified. But then I think, Oh well; it's a good thing I had two of them; I still have the boy.

"The kid's on the phone," my mother called to my father. "She has good news."

My father picks up the phone. "You're pregnant?" he says.

No. I wasn't calling to say I was pregnant, just that I'd gotten a good job. He wanted his grandchild. Who could blame him? That was what I was good for.

In fact I had been pregnant again, and again I'd wavered. Did I think I could keep my options open forever? Did I think I could still decide to be a ballerina? In the end I went back to the same doctor, but he wasn't doing abortions anymore. He thought the police were on to him. He gave me the name of another doctor.

I left his office and went home. At that time I lived in Brooklyn Heights with my second husband. Probably I stopped to do some shopping on the way home.

The next morning I went to work at my office, which was on Madison Avenue and Sixtieth Street. After work I met my husband and we went downtown to have dinner at John's Restaurant on East Twelfth Street. The next morning I went to work again. I'm not just marking time here; there's a reason I mention these mundane details. You'll see.

On the third day after my visit to the doctor's office, my husband and I took a subway, and a bus, to Fourteenth Street and Avenue B. It was a dark night and quite cold. We waited on the southwest corner of Fourteenth and B for twenty minutes or so. Eventually a man approached us. We identified ourselves and gave him some money. He led us to a nearby building and into a doctor's office, where I had an abortion. This was quite an unpleasant experience, but that's beside the point. We went right home after that. I took a week off work. A month, or even two months later, at six o'clock in the morning, we were awakened by a great banging at the door.

Police! Open up!

Now you see why I had to list all those long-ago perambulations. I'd been followed for three days—from the moment I left the first doctor's office. We'd had the bad luck to coincide with one of the periodic crackdowns on abortion which some assistant district attorney thought to ride to political office. (Years later I came out of my loft on the Bowery to the amazing spectacle of sanitation workers sweeping the street. "*What* are you *doing?*" I asked a sweeper. He inclined his head toward the far side of the Bowery. I saw the news cameras. It was an election year. "Bye-bye," said the street sweeper. "You won't see us here again.")

I really was just marking time there. Okay, here goes.

On that morning, in my little apartment on Orange Street, three big police officers filled my pretty living room. They flashed some piece of paper and actually said, "We're going downtown."

My brain was off-duty. If there was a Constitution, I didn't remember it. My husband said, "She's not going with you. She'll come later, with a lawyer."

Later, with a lawyer, I went downtown, to the office of,

let's say it was a Miss Connolly, who was an assistant D.A. Miss Connolly laid it out for me: We know everything, she said. We have photos of you entering and leaving the buildings where these *doctors* conducted their *business* (said with an accent of disgust). And, also, she said, we have ten women prepared to identify these *doctors* and testify as to their activities.

She spread an array of photographs out on her desk.

"Look at these!"

I looked. I recognized my nice doctors. Criminals, every one.

Miss Connolly said, Your lawyer will advise you that unless you testify before the grand jury, you will be arrested.

I turned to my lawyer. He shrugged. Nodded.

I made a feeble protest. "Why do you need me? You have ten other women."

Miss Connolly laughed.

In my defense, I might mention here that my husband had two young daughters and urged me to avoid publicity. That would be true enough. But let's be frank: I was afraid of jail, but more than that, *terrified* that *my* father would find out what I had done.

You don't know what you're made of until push comes to shove. Isn't that right, Daddy?

I don't tell this story very often.

In June, at the end of my sophomore year, I dropped out of Hunter College. That summer I thumbed my way across the country. I stopped off at a lumber camp in northern Montana, where I waitressed for a month, then crossed the Cascades into Washington and headed down the coast to San Francisco. It was the Summer of Love. I hung out with the Diggers in the Haight and went on the road with the Grateful Dead. After a few months of communal life I grew restless, so I took passage on a freighter bound for the South Seas. In Tahiti I was courted by a handsome prince, but I soon tired of the indolent life of the islands and took up my travels once more. Wherever I went, success and happiness awaited me. In Barcelona I studied flamenco and was celebrated as a prodigy of that art. In Vienna, where I studied opera, I became known far and wide for my talent and beauty. Riches and love were showered on me. I married a famous and wealthy left-wing writer, who had fought with the French Resistance. Together, we founded a journal to disseminate our ideas. It became very successful, read by influential people all over the world. Two perfect children, a boy and a girl, were born to us. After many years abroad I longed to see my parents again, so we flew to New York—

first class, and why not? At the airport my mother and father embraced us with tears of happiness. When their eyes fell upon their beautiful grandchildren, they almost fainted with joy.

At last they were speechless.

HOW I BECAME A WRITER

—

Do you call this serious work, darling," my mother said.

It wasn't a question.

I knew where she was coming from. I came from there myself.

—

In fact, I had been floundering. But it wasn't as if I'd just been lying around all day. I had jobs. Lots of jobs, dozens of jobs, one right after the other. I'd been a salesgirl at Macy's, been in the typing pool of an insurance company, file clerk in an advertising agency, assistant to an assistant of a television producer. Receptionist was one of my frequent occupations.

So I didn't need Mama to tell me there was a problem. She, of course, had her own ideas. Long ago, by way of piano lessons, she made it clear that she intended me to be "accomplished." ("Someday you'll thank me, darling.") For the future, she was in favor of the Law (in the interests of the downtrodden), Social Work, Teaching at the very least; not to mention the Struggle for a Better World.

Myself, I had a distinct lack of ideas, negative ideas if you like. Not the Law, not Social Work, definitely not Teaching. As for the Struggle, it was just as well for It that it proceed without me. Not that It wasn't in the back of my mind *all* the time; I knew this because everything else the world offered seemed beside the point, and every moment of every day, the sense of a great mission refused rang in my head like tinnitus.

So, given the circumstances, you can see the problem: how to reconcile the high seriousness of "accomplishment," and of fighting for social and economic justice, with my evidently selfish and frivolous nature.

Mama said to take an aptitude test. I scored high on love of animals. Veterinarian? Why not? I would be called "Dr." And surely the welfare of animals was part of the struggle for a better world. But wait. I was forgetting something: Didn't I drop Biology 101 the moment I was handed the frog and scalpel? Absolutely nothing occurred to me at that moment except to register at yet another employment agency.

The ladies who ran Career Blazers were easy. They didn't seem to mind that I couldn't *do* anything, could hardly type, could not take shorthand beyond *if u cn rd th u cn gt a gd jb.* And they didn't laugh out loud when I said I wanted a Creative Job or a Job Helping People. They kept getting me the same sorts of jobs I'd been getting by myself, and I kept quitting or being fired. And because they didn't throw up their hands, I kept coming back to them. Finally they did roll their eyes; but instead of saying, Go away and learn to *do* something! they said, Well, you can work for us. And they didn't even charge me a fee.

So for a while I answered phones at Career Blazers, taking listings for jobs on offer; if a job seemed interesting, I got first crack at the interview. And one day I answered a call for the job of my life.

"I have just the candidate for you," I said. "She'll be at your office in an hour."

That was how I came to be a writer. And this is the lead paragraph of the first thing I ever wrote: *Steve McQueen drove his motorcycle through the rain-slicked streets of the Village and skidded to a stop in front of Louie's Bar. He could imagine his friends inside, laughing, smoking, drinking beer. How could he face them?*

I was a natural! So I said, "Mama. I'm going to be a writer!" She glanced at the covers of *Screen Stars* and *Movie World,* and *that's* when she said, "Do you call this serious work, darling."

—

Whatever. I began work at Magazine Management Company, where magazines were produced the way Detroit produced cars. I worked on the fan-magazine line. On the other side of a four-foot partition was the romance line. Across a corridor was the men's line. Also, there was a comic-book line.

All these "books," as I learned to call them, were the property of Mr. Goodman (no first-name bonhomie with him), who was a skinflint and something of a sadist. He maintained authority by displays of rage, and by humiliating his editors; he also had the sadist's trick of sometimes being really nice.

For a pittance (eighty dollars a week to start), Mr. Goodman hired writers with lots of talent and no money, or writers with less talent and even less money. He collected has-beens and soon-to-bes; the desperate, the bitter, the hopeful, the alcoholic, the extremely eccentric, the flotsam of society. Nothing in my experience had prepared me for such interesting colleagues. Neither was I prepared for hilarity on the job.

Such as the snowy winter night when four or five guys—editors, writers—went to Central Park. Once in the park, an editor put on snowshoes and made footprints in the snow. An assistant took pictures as a writer dashed into nearby bushes. In the resulting photograph you could just make out an ominous blurred figure obscured by brush and the large footprints the running creature left behind. The next cover of *Stag* features the headline: BIGFOOT CAPTURED ON FILM! and the story, certified to be true, tells of a brave adventurer who trekked the Himalayas in search of the legendary being.

Because we were all so poorly paid, we earned extra money by selling stories to other books. Several times I tried to write for a romance book. "He unbuttoned her blouse, and her breasts fell out." It wasn't just me. Writers with honest-to-God real books to their credit would turn out sentences like "Toward dusk, the river widened . . . I opened the glove compartment and in a second I was inside."

I never mastered the romance story, but by some odd

brain chemistry I had an immediate instinct for the fans. After I had read a few and written a few, I just *knew*. At last, I had a Creative Job.

———

A short tour of Magazine Management: It is, let's say, six months after I have started the job. I arrive at the office at nine o'clock. In the small reception area, I greet the switchboard operator. (My status is scarcely more exalted than hers; I relieve her at the switchboard three lunch hours a week.) Chatting up the pretty operator is tall, handsome Bruce Jay Friedman, who will be famous very soon. (Even after he publishes his novel *Stern* to critical acclaim, he does not feel free to call Mr. Goodman by his first name.)

And here, passing through the alcove that holds the heart of our operation—six large file cabinets containing every word published anywhere about every star and starlet—is short, squat Mario Puzo. He is working on a novel about the Mafia, he says, which he hopes will make him some money.

A few years ago, Mickey Spillane could be seen in these halls, and a few years after I leave, Martin Cruz Smith will put in his time. For now it is literary excitement enough to see Leicester Hemingway, Ernest's brother, pop in from time to time to collect his checks for fishing stories.

These are the famous and the near famous. But now here

is George Penty in his cubicle. He will never exactly be famous, but no one who has met him will ever forget him. Southern gentry, champion drinker; his conversation is conducted entirely in winks, nods, allusions, innuendos, ellipses. And George was brave enough to have been a labor organizer in parts of the country run by the Klan, although how the workers ever organized on his instructions is beyond me.

And, in the next cubicle, barking into the telephone, is the most exotic plant of all, Therese Pol, product of a one-night alliance between an Ohio piano teacher studying in Berlin and the German composer Paul Dessau. Poor Therese: her mother ran back home, leaving her in the Europe between the wars, farmed out with anyone who'd take her. Therese made her way: in Paris, as a lover of Lawrence Durrell, who used her as a model for Justine; as a translator of Wilhelm Reich and Dürrenmatt; as a writer of a few pieces for *The New Yorker*; as a great beauty. That was then. Now Therese is a ruin. Alcohol, barbiturates, and, it is rumored, a lobotomy. Still, her tongue is caustic; and she is possessed of a Teutonic obsession for accuracy, determined to make the fantasies published in *Hunting Adventures* conform to fact.

What is she saying on the telephone now?

"Tell me!" she demands of some bemused herpetologist. "Can a tarantula grow to thirty feet? . . . No? Well, how big *can* it grow? . . . Does it sun itself with its mate? . . ."

———

These are a few of my colleagues. Among them I will find a best friend, I will find love (many find love in this institution, if only for a week or two), even a husband (a second husband). But now to work.

Marge is my editor. She is throning it behind a glass partition. (In not many months, I will be throning it there myself.) I sit down at my desk outside her tiny office, one of the four desks reserved for writers of the fan magazines. And then, on this typical day, I begin to think about Elizabeth Taylor.

Let me make this plain. We had almost no access to the stars we wrote about. The big ones got all the publicity they wanted in real magazines. And even when, on occasion, a desperate starlet granted an interview, nothing resembling a secret was confided. Mostly we made things up.

Elizabeth Taylor's life is a gift to us. Events galore! Scandals one after the other, disasters right and left. But the events of her life, rapidly as they occur, still do not keep pace with the schedule of a bimonthly; and after I have written innumerable stories about how she has stolen Eddie Fisher—

the best friend of her late husband Mike Todd—from Debbie Reynolds (*Debbie may forget in time, but Debbie's babies will remember forever. Elizabeth Taylor is the woman who deprived them of their father, of a normal childhood. How will Liz be able to face her own children?*), and about how, not content with that, the hussy is *now* dumping Eddie for Richard Burton, is it possible to angle *another* fifteen-hundred-word piece with nothing but these same elements?

Some photographs are on my desk. Elizabeth Taylor pictured with each of her husbands. With Nicky Hilton, with Michael Wilding, with Mike Todd, with Eddie Fisher; and one taken just a few days earlier with Richard Burton. I stare at the pictures hoping for inspiration . . . and idly notice that Elizabeth's left hand appears in each picture. Various wedding rings can be seen. Interesting. I get out a magnifying glass. Whoa! Hold on! In the photograph with Burton, she's wearing what looks to be a wedding ring, but it is *not* the ring Eddie married her with. There's my story! Are LIZ AND DICK SECRETLY MARRIED? That I know the answer is no does not deter me for a moment.

Mrs. Eddie Fisher is wearing a new wedding ring these days, a thin platinum band, distinctly different from the wide gold ring Debbie's ex-husband put on her finger when they vowed eternal love. . . . In the second paragraph I switch to the tense in which, in the absence of any facts, much of what we produce is written.

As she held out her hand for Burton to slip the narrow band on her finger, the ring that held the promise that one day they would be truly wed, Liz must have thought of the past, as well as the future. How often over the years had she held out her hand in just this way? And each time, hadn't she believed that this *time was different,* this *time would be forever?*

And then I pull out her clipping file and fill out the rest of the piece with the well-known story of her life to date, documented by her own contemporary quotes: *"I adore him," Liz said, gazing at her new husband* [Nicky, Michael, Mike, Eddie]. *"We're so happy; we're going to grow old together."* The story will be illustrated with these very photographs, the telltale rings circled. If I say so myself, it is a stroke of genius, and everybody, from my editor to Mr. Goodman, agrees.

———

That's what I did from nine to five. Of course I didn't write nonstop. We had to keep the clipping files up-to-date. That meant reading all the other fan magazines and the gossip columns and scouring respectable magazines and newspapers. Whether or not what they reported was any more accurate than what we invented was of no matter. We also had to buy photographs of the stars from what are now called the paparazzi. We had to paste up the entire magazine and cut the stories to fit. We had to write cover titles, captions, and blurbs.

In this fashion Earth orbited more than three times, and long before this time had passed, I could single-handedly put out an entire magazine, from written word to layout.

Those years were full of professional excitements. Like the time Elizabeth Taylor sued all the fan magazines for several million dollars and Mr. Goodman told us we'd better change our tune. I wrote: *"The fog was thick in London that early Sunday morning. Liz clutched her mink coat tightly as she walked the half-remembered streets of her childhood."* Soon she meets a little girl who is out on her own. Liz stops to speak to her. She discovers that the child, whose name, by an odd chance, is also Elizabeth, lives in an orphanage, the orphanage of St. Agnes. In the course of the story, Liz makes a sizable gift to the orphanage (the single tiny kernel of fact that informs almost all our stories). And thus, in the course of a month, Elizabeth Taylor makes a quick switch from THE WOMAN MEN HATE TO LOVE to THE ANGEL OF ST. AGNES. As I wrote the dialogue between the big and the little Elizabeth, tears rolled down my cheeks.

Also during those years the Disney studios granted me an interview with Annette Funicello. I was not an experienced interviewer, so I followed the style of a previous editor known for shock tactics. In a telephone interview with an actor, this woman had been overheard asking, "Nick, when you go on a date, do you think the boy or the girl should be responsible for the contraception?"

"Annette," I said. "I think our readers would be interested in knowing why you had your nose fixed."

"I *didn't* have my nose fixed," Annette snarled. "I had an operation for a deviated septum." Unbidden, the title flashed through my mind: ANNETTE'S NIGHT OF HORROR: THE TERRIBLE THING THAT STOPPED HER BREATH.

And Mai Britt, a stunning blond Swedish actress, was briefly married to Sammy Davis, Jr. This marriage was a delicate matter. A number of our competitors finessed the issue with cover stories along the line of "How Will Mai and Sammy Explain Their Love to Their Children?" But hadn't I been raised in a tradition so insistent on color blindness that when you wanted, for instance, to point out the sole black person in a group of whites, you were forced to say, "He's the guy with the blue sweater and brown pants."? So, while I acknowledged that there was a social problem inherent in this mating, it was different from the one you might expect:

"I love him," said Mai Britt. "I know there are differences between us. Some people will never understand why I married a man shorter than I am."

—

When Marge left, I took my courage in both hands and went to Mr. Goodman. It needed courage, believe me. Strong men tossed back double martinis to prepare themselves for the ordeal of explaining to Mr. Goodman why sales figures were not up to par.

"Why should I give *you* the job?" said Mr. Goodman.

"Because I think I can do it."

"You *think* you can do it?"

Mr. Goodman stared at me for a long moment. "Okay. Let's see."

Things went along swimmingly for a while. I started an advice column, "Talk It Over with Nan Tyler," and vouched for Nan's reality by running a photograph of our bookkeeper at the top of the column. I hardly need to say that we wrote all the letters as well as the answers. I also sent *Movie World*'s special correspondent to Hollywood, so that she could renew her personal friendships with the stars and bring back news straight from their mouths. To document this event I had a photograph taken of myself, the editor, at my desk, shaking the switchboard operator's hand in bon voyage.

But all good things come to an end. One day a photographer brought me some pictures of Connie Stevens to choose among for a cover. I bought one for the following issue of *Screen Stars*. Connie, all flirtatious smiles, leaned back against a tree. The cover was printed, the magazine bound and shipped and, just as the issue was about to go on sale, someone noticed a carving on the tree: MARY SUCKS BLACK COCK. *You* try explaining that to Mr. Goodman.

So that was that. I didn't mind. It was time to go. I'd learned just about everything there was to learn. And I had this strange feeling. I wanted to do some serious work.

BY THE BOOK

—

I saw an ad in the paper. Bowery loft. Sunny. 1,000 sq. ft. 199/mo.

I was looking for an apartment. Two hundred a month was exactly what I'd had in mind.

—

A little-publicized aspect of happiness is being in the condition of not having to look in the classifieds. Not for a job, not for an apartment, surely not for love. For a number of years I'd been well situated in Brooklyn Heights. I had a darling apartment, the whole top floor of a very small building on Orange Street, which is sandwiched prettily between Pineapple and Cranberry. The house was owned by a family of Jehovah's Witnesses. They lived on the lower two floors and always peered into the hallway when I came home. No doubt to see if I was sneaking a man home. I was sorry to disappoint them so often.

What I still miss about that apartment is the bathroom. It was a comparatively large room, as large as the living room. I kept a dressing table and chair in it, and on winter Sundays I'd get into the old claw-foot tub, which was right beside a sunny window, and stay there reading for hours, not anwering the doorbell when the Jehovahs rang to proselytize. This may have been why, when my lease was up, the Jehovahs gave my apartment to their own kind. So, back to the classifieds.

By this time I was a twice-divorced woman with an extant broken heart due to a recent romance. Plus, I was sick of my job. I'd been working at a women's magazine—oh, let's name it: *Redbook*—as an editor in the articles department. If socio-porn were a category, it would describe most of these articles. DOES ADULTERY ENHANCE MARRIAGE? A SOCIOLOGIST SURVEYS 10,000 WOMEN. . . . OLDER MEN, YOUNGER WOMEN? A

SYMPOSIUM. (It was odd—some might say ironic, but they would be wrong—that the experts always answered these questions with a resounding affirmative. I sometimes wondered if my boss's wife had ever been scientifically surveyed; if so, did she know about her husband's young secretary, who was quite a cute little number?) Anyway, my life was definitely not going according to plan. And just what was this plan, please?

—

The reason I couldn't pay more than two hundred dollars a month for an apartment is that I was quitting my job to make my way as a freelance writer. These days, you couldn't get your overhead low enough to take the chance. These days, you'd be lucky if two hundred dollars was all you had to pay for dinner at a fashionable Bowery club. *If* you could get in. In the days I'm talking about, the Bowery was still your basic, if world-class, skid row, and the Lower East Side was where your penniless grandmother had to live when she first came to this country.

I was a little nervous about the neighborhood, so I took my friend Liz with me when I went to see the loft. We started from Bleecker Street, walking down the west side of the Bowery. It was summer. The heat was infernal. The smell of urine and vomit seemed to hang just at nostril level. We stepped over bodies, detoured around them. Here and there arms reached for us; if not for that, I'd have sworn most of the guys of the sidewalk were dead. *Can I do this?*

The building, 215 Bowery, was on the northeast corner of the Bowery and Rivington Street. We stood across the street looking at it: dark brown stone, five very tall stories high, with a cash-register store on the ground floor. The entrance was on the Bowery; the rest of the building wrapped around the corner.

"Look!" said Liz. "A doorman." ("Just drag my doorman out of the doorway," I instructed visitors for the next decade.) We crossed the street, coaxed the prone body out of the way, and climbed to the third floor. A guy opened the door. The place of my dreams. Really.

Empty, and flooded with light. Pressed-tin ceilings thirteen feet high. Seven windows, each one ten feet tall, faced south onto Rivington Street. Unobstructed, the sun poured in. Three more windows faced west across the Bowery, with a view of three doll-sized, dormered Federal houses.

At the eastern end of the loft, the previous tenant had horizontally bisected an alcove: a room-sized closet below, a sleeping platform above. Except for that, the space was open. The eye took in everything at once. I had no doubt. This was my place. I could see my life here.

Except, possibly, it could use some redecoration. The narrow plank floors had been painted black; I'd repaint in pale putty. White for the walls and ceiling. Get rid of the blackout shades. The couch goes at the far end, the table over there, the desk over here . . . I climbed the wooden ladder leading from the closet to the bedroom. The space was large enough to hold a double bed, a small chest, a chair. I could stand up if I slumped a bit.

From the south window where I intended to put my desk there was a view across Rivington Street of One Mile House, a decaying three-story bar/flophouse, built on the site of the old mile-marker from City Hall. Through all the years I looked across the street, a rag mop hung from the same third-floor window. In the early mornings, when I sat down at my desk, the sun lit up One Mile House. Every detail of shadowed windows, peeling paint, and crumbling bricks, every strand of the mop, was thrown into brilliant relief. The sight filled my window like a life-sized Hopper.

On some nights, the room across from my desk remained dark, but on many nights, a bare ceiling bulb switched on. Then I saw a scrawny old man (maybe always the same man) sitting in his underwear on a narrow metal bed. Sometimes he sat with his head in his hands, sometimes he walked around the room; from time to time he looked toward my window. In this way many a New Year's Eve passed.

———

"You're going to live *here*, darling?" my mother said.

Anybody's mother would be dubious: no real bathroom, no kitchen sink, no air-conditioning, hardly any heat, the neighborhood, the drunks, the seemingly downward social slide.

"And, darling," she said. "So much noise!"

She meant the music, piped in by loudspeaker from the Dominican social club across the street. At that particular moment, the summer's favorite happened to be playing: *I'll be thereeee / before the neeeext / teardrop faaallls . . .*

But Daddy. He was thrilled: the rent, the lack of amenities, the badly needed repairs. He liked the style. It was *his* style. He had me at his mercy.

"You need a kitchen sink," he said. "Good. I got a sink for you."

He ripped out the old hand basin, left over from the time when the place was a sewing loft, and put in an elderly kitchen sink, which he must have found by the side of a road.

"Let's see the bathroom."

Bathroom? Two narrow side-by-side doors, the original toilet stalls for the workers. (I knew the place had once been a garment shop, because some needles were still embedded between the narrow floorboards.) One door opened to the surviving toilet; the second toilet had been converted into a makeshift shower. The floors were rough concrete. Did Daddy have some tiles stashed somewhere?

He flushed the toilet. "Good enough," he said, meaning the water pressure.

He eyed the ladder to the sleeping loft. "It's *fine*, Daddy."

"We'll see," he said.

"Heat?"

There was actually one small radiator, but mainly there was the stove, a potbellied wood-burning stove.

"Ah!" he said. It made him glad. He knew what a stove needed: wood. *There* was a job without end. Over the years he brought me wood: scavenged wood from building sites, wood coated with creosote, thus adding immeasurably to the danger of a chimney fire; wood full of rusted nails that could give you tetanus if you handled it carelessly and that sounded like Fourth of July cherry bombs when it burned.

I was all set. Now what?

———

No more nine to five, no more regular paychecks—I was going to be a writer. What kind of a writer remained to be seen. For a few years I traveled around the country chasing stories: I lived in a whorehouse in Nevada for five days. Not exactly *in* the whorehouse but in a small, freezing shack out back; in their off-hours, I talked to the whores. ("What's a nice girl like you . . . ?" Will it surprise you to learn they did it for the money?) I went to California to write a story about a woman whose arms were eaten off by a bear. I went to Idaho to write about the collapse of the Teton Dam. I was on a jury that tried a murder case, and I wrote about that. I went to the Yakima Valley to write a piece about a ninety-nine-year-old woman and five very much alive generations of her female descendants. An editor asked me to expand that piece into a book, and for a couple of years I worked on that.

My darling daughter,

I have been remembering that when you wrote about Elizabeth Taylor, I said that I didn't think that a serious magazine would print the article. My dear daughter, I hurt your feelings, but I know that you have forgiven me. If you hadn't I would have been eating my heart out all these years. How ignorant I was of what it takes to "create." I should have known better . . . Daddy and I are very proud of you, even if Daddy has never mentioned it . . .

So, evidently, I wasn't a total loss. I'd written a book. Mind you, not a book I felt deeply attached to; it hadn't been *my* idea, after all, but it was a respectable book, one that made my mother, even my father, proud. (As it happened, it met the fate of many respectable books; it fell into a Black Hole. I say this with no bitterness. Bitterness comes later.) I was agreeably surprised to have produced a book. I liked the perks, among them having Mama eat her words. And it seems I was having a career. Not brilliant, but I was working steadily, meeting deadlines, seeing my words in print. No rejections, no kill fees. Not bad.

And with success came the idea that I could write *another* book. I had a subject. Doesn't every writer make use of his history? What was my history? Wasn't it History itself?

Oh, but this was getting serious. I was thinking of taking on the very story of Communism. And much more. Because how can you separate Communism from everything else going on? So, let's assume here that I'm even capable of researching and mastering so immense a body of factual material. What organizing principle would sustain such a book? It was *so* complicated, *so* many strands weaving back and forth through *so* many years, leading in *so* many directions, to *so* many actors, *so* many events. It was too much to comprehend! . . . Too complicated! . . . Impossible! . . . Out of the question! . . . I'd just forget the whole thing. Who would know that I had shirked the one piece of work that was necessary to me?

And here fate takes a hand. One summer evening, I went to a dinner party. It was a lively evening; interesting conversation took place. By dessert, I saw my way. A few days later I went to the library to see what I could find out about an obscure, murdered, Italian-born anarchist named Carlo Tresca. Not so many days after that, I proposed a biography of Carlo Tresca to a prominent and famously boyish editor at a very classy publishing house.

Terrific idea, he said. Sign here.

—

I know what you're saying now: Carlo *who?* Multitudes would say the same. Never mind.

From his birth in 1879, in the mountain village of Sulmona, in the Abruzzi, until his murder in 1943, on Fifth Avenue and Fifteenth Street, I tracked Carlo Tresca. Luck had been with me when, knowing almost nothing about him, I chose him; and luck stayed with me.

Lucky for me he was murdered: What more satisfying design for a book than a murder mystery?

Lucky for me he was a man with a gift for making friends: His friendships were deep, ranged widely, and represented every political current on the left.

Lucky for me he had a talent for making enemies—the right enemies: Mussolini was one of his very personal enemies; others embodied the rising ideologies of Communism and Fascism.

Lucky for me he was Italian: He had dealings with the Mafia, and we know how inherently interesting the Mafia is.

Lucky for me he was a womanizer: Nothing like love affairs to spice up history.

Luckiest of all, he was an anarchist. That was *exactly* the perspective I needed to see through the rousing slogans, the marching songs, through the exhortations to the proletariat (all of which had clouded my brain), and into the dark heart of Soviet Communism. Carlo Tresca was my long-deferred education in History, writ large and personal. I could hardly believe my luck!

—

I worked on research for many years. Documents had to be wrested from government agencies that seemed to exist for the very purpose of preventing me from seeing what was in their files. But I was very diligent, very persistent; by and large I got what I needed. I began with a two-drawer file cabinet; I added a four-drawer cabinet and every drawer was crammed full. You could say I became obsessed with my project, even a little mad. For one thing, I worried a *lot* about a guy in Illinois who was, I learned, also working on a biography of Tresca. Eventually I got his name. An Italian name—*not* a good sign. I dug a little deeper. His *father* had known Tresca. Oh, God; this guy had the inside track. I called the guy up.

Tresca! he said. Why are *you* doing Tresca? Do you know *anything* about the anarchist movement? Do you speak Italian, do you read Italian?

Not exactly, I said with some exaggeration.

He laughed. Oh, go right ahead then, he said. I'm almost finished; I'm working on my last chapter.

(Dear Reader, as I write so many years later, he hasn't yet finished. Not long after *I* had finished, we appeared together on a panel. I have to admit it, the guy knew his stuff. He was deeply knowledgeable. And when he had concluded his erudite remarks, he smiled at the audience and turned to me: "Dorothy," he said, "will now discuss Carlo Tresca's love life." Really! Had I made a dime, I would have cried all the way to the bank.)

Not only did I expend a lot of energy worrying about my rival, I also worried about robbery, and about fire destroying my files. I could *do* something about that: I bought a fireproof safe and kept my most important papers in it.

Now, everything I have just related is proof of the adage that the things you worry about are not the things that happen. As far as the safe was concerned, I might better have put myself in it, for now enters a real danger.

He arrives by telephone. A stranger. He's interested in my subject, he says. Can we meet and talk?

Of course. Delighted. So pleased to talk about my obscure subject. Not many are interested. And this guy turns out to be quite attractive. Soon he's giving every indication that he's interested in me as well.

Dinner? Why not? So much to talk about.

Well. After a few dinners, and the rest of it, he wonders if he can borrow some portion of my files for a paper he's giving at some academic conference having to do with an aspect of our mutual work.

Here, as they say, I hesitate visibly. *You* know how I feel about these documents. But this attractive guy seems quite annoyed by my reluctance. He speaks—almost sharply—about the obligations of collegiality and scholarly generosity. He makes reference to our burgeoning romance. He is, if he says so himself, sincerely hurt by my evident distrust.

Yes! Indeed! He walks off with a portion of my hard-won files and I never hear from him again.

—

A diversion, merely. I am inexorably on my path. Eight years after I began work, my book was finished. Then my luck really ran out.

Dear Dorothy [wrote my editor, famous worldwide for his literary discernment],

I'm sorry to have to tell you . . . don't know what to say . . . would like to help you but . . . so badly written that . . . unpublishable . . . rewritten from beginning to end . . . even so, can't see how it can ever . . .

Depressed? No, not depressed. Shamed. Paralyzed with shame. *Avoid shame,* reads the inscription on a gravestone somewhere in England. *People must not be humiliated,* says Chekhov. I was *so* ashamed that I could not pick up my clothes at the dry cleaner. How could I? The dry cleaner had the idea that I was a writer. Walk the dog? Some other dog walker might ask how my book was going. (Eight years of walking the dog is a long time; you have to say something.) See friends? Go to a party? I could barely buy a quart of milk.

At last, after two long years in this wilderness, a university press took my manuscript.

Reviews began to appear:

A first-class book . . . a perfect detective story . . . brings back a whole period in American life. . . . Important but neglected figure. . . . Exciting. . . . Absorbing. . . . Fine in-

*vestigative work ... chilling historical insights. ... Im-
mensely interesting ...*

On the Thursday night before the Sunday when a full-
page, glowing (if I may say so) review of my book would
appear in the *Times Book Review,* I went to somebody else's
book party. (See how much better I was feeling?) In the
lobby, boarding the elevator with me, was my erstwhile editor. I trembled; or shivered. I positioned myself at his side.
Shoulder to shoulder we stood, facing front.

"Bob," I said to the elevator door. "What a *terrible* letter
you wrote me."

"Really?" he said. Behind his large horn-rimmed glasses,
I could imagine his eyebrows lifting in surprise. "I'm so *surprised* to hear you say so," he said. "Why, I have drawerfuls
of letters from writers thanking me for my tact."

"I don't think so," I said. "Just possibly, you have *drawers*ful."

And what was that? A pinprick when I longed for a sledge-
hammer. Pathetic, right? But, and maybe you'll agree, a
writerly weapon nevertheless.

SOCIAL HISTORY

—

I happened to be at home when Rose phoned. I saw my mother pick up the phone, listen. I saw her clap her hand to her mouth. I heard her say angrily, "We begged her to move. *Didn't* we beg her? She was so *stubborn!*"

Clara Isserman, widow of my father's best friend, had been found dead, found murdered, in the apartment where she had lived for almost thirty years.

I hadn't been in that building or neighborhood since I was a kid, but I remembered it pretty well. It was in the East Bronx. A lot of our friends and relatives lived in the East Bronx. You got to the East Bronx on the El, riding above an interminable shadowed and light-slashed street. Looking out the window of the train, you saw fragments of life in the apartment windows at eye level: dirty, limp curtains flapping, potted plants dying, forty-watt bulbs hanging from ceiling cords. Sometimes you looked right into the face of a tenant leaning from a sixth-floor window.

Really poor people lived in the buildings that lined the El. On either side of the tracks the more advantaged lived, on street after street of soot-stained five-, six-, seven-story tenements. These streets stretched as far as you could see: the concrete sidewalks, the stone buildings; I don't remember any trees. There weren't many sights to lift the spirits in the East Bronx, but in those days the housing was still intact, the rents were cheap, and landlords were required to paint your apartment every three years. In those days, there was work in small manufacturing companies nearby. In those days, there was a working class, and this was one of their neighborhoods. We lived in a neighborhood very much like it in Washington Heights.

The Issermans lived several blocks from the El, in a building at the top of a hilly street. They had a view that was almost a vista of vacant weed- and brush-filled lots. On long-ago Sundays, we often went to visit Clara and Yitzak and, in time, their daughter, Toby.

—

The men talk in the living room, and I follow my mother and Clara into the kitchen. In a high-pitched singsong (a soprano that is heartbreakingly beautiful when I hear her sing Yiddish songs on the radio), Clara lists her husband's derelictions. *He doesn't care for me . . . he doesn't do what he promises . . . he gives too much money to the Cause . . . he spoils the child . . . he turns the child against me . . .* My mother listens patiently, protesting from time to time, but Clara is unstoppable. She is filled with grievance. *You think he's so good, you don't know him!*

But he *is* good. He is slight, bald, and, as far as I can tell, deeply sweet in his nature. He is a housepainter by trade, a decorator and builder when he gets the chance. He is my father's best friend. They are boyhood friends. They are *landsmen*. They even share a name: Yitzak. Yitzak Isserman is the one person who knew and loved my father in that unimaginable distant past, in that unimaginable distant place. He is the one who shows me my father:

Your grandfather was a tanner in our town. Lomazy. He was a hard man, a strict man. Very strict. Sometimes, and not so seldom, he would beat your daddy, because, to tell the truth, your daddy was a little wild. Like what? Like the trick he played on the old blind man. Well, never mind.

Your zayde made your daddy work in the tannery. It was a terrible place. Such a stink! But also Zayde wanted a rabbi in the family for the honor of it, and your daddy was supposed to study to become a rabbi. To say the least, he was no scholar, but don't say I told you. They had a lot of fights.

All of us boys dreamed of America. Your daddy was the first to go. He had courage. One day he just disappeared. I knew his plan. He took some money Zayde had hidden in the barn. And then, knowing that Zayde would send some-one to find him, he played a trick. (The truth is, he was al-ways playing tricks.) He took the train to Warsaw. From Warsaw, he sent a letter home: "Don't look for me. I'm going to Rotterdam to take the boat for America." Instead, he got on a train to Hamburg and took the ship from there.

Even so, he was almost caught. A fellow townsman recognized him on the train.

"Aren't you Yitzak Rosenbloom?"

"No," your daddy said. "I'm Yitzak Isserman." (He always thought quickly.)

"Really? Do you know that Yitzak Rosenbloom ran away from home?"

"I don't believe it!" said your daddy. "He would have told me. He's my best friend!"

The friends lost track of each other for more than a decade. Then one day, crossing one of those light-slashed streets under the El, they found each other.

"*Yitzak!*" they cried with joy.

Boyhood had passed; they were men approaching thirty, with more adventures behind them than they would have the rest of their lives.

In a luncheonette under the El, with trains periodically drowning his words, Isserman tells his story. He had joined the Socialist Bund in Poland. After the revolution in Russia, he became active with the Communists. The authorities cracked down and he fled to Germany, where the revolution was soon expected. When the uprising failed, he was thrown in jail. And there he languished until Clara, who had been in love with him in their hometown, who had followed him to Germany despite his indifference to her, managed to get him released. She was very tenacious—you had to give her that. And also, she was musically gifted.

"So," Isserman said, "we got married."

My father remembered Clara. "So. You married her."

My father's story had its drama, too. The steerage passage from Hamburg to America, ending not in New York but in Galveston. What a place! Hot as hell! His first job: driving a horse and a wagon filled with bananas to sell to farmers on outlying farms; on the road for a week at a time, sleeping in barns when he got permission, sometimes eating nothing but bananas. I'm sure he told the story of how, one evening, with his few words of English, he asked a farmwife, "Can I sleep with you tonight?"

And after a few years in Texas, he is rescued. A train ticket to Philadelphia arrives from a friend, his one friend in America, a fellow passenger on the ship that brought them. In Philadelphia there were people who spoke his language, and factory jobs that began before dawn; beds in boardinghouses shared with someone on the night shift; onion sandwiches for lunch; $1.50 for a meal ticket that bought a week's dinners. And, yes, he had met a girl in Philadelphia. He, too, was a married man, eight years now.

No, no children (and not for another eight years). Now he was a laundryman. All day he drove a truck, picking up dirty laundry and delivering wet wash. Up the tenement stairs carrying the heavy loads of wash on his back, calling, *Wet wash! Wet wash!*

So after these long years of wandering, here they were in the Bronx, each with a best friend again.

——

Seven or eight years after I was born, Isserman and Clara had Toby. "You were their inspiration," my mother said. "Be a sister to her."

Not a chance. First of all, I liked not having a sister; second, I never liked Toby. From the first, she was a disagreeable, imperious child, her face always screwed up, about to wail, and when she began to talk she had her mother's high, complaining voice. Toby was smart, all right; she knew how to play mother against father, and she grew up willful and with no charm that I ever noticed. Isserman adored and spoiled her, Clara shrieked at both of them.

Isserman died of a heart attack when he was not much more than sixty. To everyone's consternation, my father, who never showed feeling, wept. By that time Toby must have been close to twenty. She had moved out of Ward Avenue a couple of years before, to live on the Lower East Side.

And now, without Isserman to mediate, the battles between mother and daughter grew fiercer. Toby demanded money: *It was my father's money, he wanted me to have it.* Clara withheld: *When you finish school . . . when you stop hanging around with those degenerates . . . when you start treating me with some respect.*

I would hear about this from my mother, from Rose. They'd roll their eyes despairingly: "Only in America," they'd say. For Isserman's sake, they kept in touch with Clara.

Eventually Toby moved to California. We heard that she married, then that a child had been born. So Toby was growing up, settling down; Clara sent money. But after a few years we heard of some troubles, unspecified. Clara told my mother that the grandparents were raising the child. This was the last straw; she had made it clear to Toby, she told my mother, that no more money would be forthcoming.

Clara stayed on in the apartment on Ward Avenue. She continued to sing in the Yiddish chorus, and once in a while, I heard her on WNYC, her voice as sweet and pure as ever. But she was bitter, getting old, and she was very lonely. The neighborhood had changed: With muggings and burglaries ever more common, Clara's nearby friends, like Rose, grew fearful and fled. Everyone urged Clara to move, but, as my mother said, she was stubborn.

And then she did decide to move. To California. Who else did she have in the world but Toby? And now a grandson. She began to pack up her apartment; in the lobby of her building, she put up a notice of household goods for sale.

A few days before Clara was to leave, she and Rose made a date for a farewell lunch. When Clara didn't show up, Rose telephoned. No answer that afternoon, no answer that evening, no answer the next morning. "I feared the worst," said Rose, although the worst turned out to be something she couldn't imagine. So she called the police and went with them to Clara's apartment. The door was unlocked. They found Clara in a half-filled bathtub, dressed only in a bra and panties, floating facedown. No accident, the police said.

Toby came east for the funeral. I saw her for the first time in years. She looked the same. We exchanged a few words: *How terrible . . . I'm so sorry . . . yes it was horrible . . . no the police don't have a clue.*

—

Years passed, and I thought about Clara from time to time. I thought about the manner of her death, which had so shocked everyone, but really no one had mourned her, certainly not as her husband had been mourned. She was nobody's beloved and she knew it. I thought about moments that must have redeemed her life: that long-ago day, for instance, when, having managed to get Isserman released from prison, she knew that she had won him—that day, she must have been triumphantly happy. And her music, singing would have brought elation; pregnancy, the birth of her daughter—before she knew how badly that lottery would turn out. Her last moments didn't bear thinking about at all.

Ah, but I was thinking about it; and what I thought was: Why waste good material? I had an idea that I could use Clara's life and death as an occasion for a high-class piece of social history. I could see it in *Harper's*, or *The Atlantic*: the changing demographics of a Bronx neighborhood, a once stable working-class community slipping into decay and disorder as the local economy declined and jobs fled; the population shift to black and Hispanic—all of it leading inevitably to the moment when a dark stranger knocked on Clara Isserman's door, knowing that an old, defenseless white woman had a little money from the sale of household goods.

When I called the local police precinct and said I wanted to talk to them about Clara Isserman's murder, the detective was quite accommodating. Anytime, he said. In fact, he said, I'll have a squad car meet you at the station. I did think that was a little odd.

I rode the El up to the Bronx. Not much had changed. I remembered those limp curtains and dying plants, the forty-watt bulbs, the tired faces peering from sixth-floor-walk-up windows. At the end of the line, the promised squad car waited. And in a small room, entirely filled up by three detectives, I began to ask my questions. Except it was soon evident that I was not in charge.

What was your relation to the deceased? . . . Didn't you say that she was your aunt? . . . She wasn't exactly your aunt? . . . How close are you to her daughter? . . . When were you last in touch with her? . . . Do you know her husband? . . . Do you recognize the person in this picture?

I was handed a glossy black-and-white photograph in which I recognized, *barely* recognized, Toby. Her face was bruised and swollen. Her eyes stared blankly into the lens. Printed on her chest was a series of numbers. Let me tell you, I was stunned! Evidently, Toby had a record—allegedly for selling drugs, for prostitution. For the police, it was a routine assumption that this small-time-criminal history could lead to murder. According to their scenario, it was possible that Toby, or her husband, or both of them—desperate characters—had come east to get money from Clara. They would have had a key to the apartment, and surprised a half-dressed Clara. There was a fight. Tempers flared. Clara was hit on the head. To confuse evidence, they put Clara's body in the bathtub.

I asked about the evidence. None, really. Just a vaguely reported sighting of a young white male in Clara's building at the requisite time. Not nearly enough to justify the expense of sending a detective to California to question Toby. Hence the hospitality of a squad car to me. Would I write to Toby and invite her to New York?

I said, No, we're not on those terms. I said, Sure, I'll let you know if I ever hear that Toby is in New York.

———

I took the El and went home. As you can imagine I was quite dejected. How in the world could I write my social history without a dark stranger?

THE LAST INDIAN

—

Yes, almost all of them were gone, and yet I saw them everywhere. *There goes another one of my dead*, I'd think as I watched an old woman hauling herself onto a kneeling bus. Struggling down the block with heavy shopping bags. In a wheelchair, pushed by a minder. Is that my daddy beetling along in his plaid loggers' cap? Uncle Oscar standing in the courtesy line at the bank? My own mama, teetering on the curb, stretching out a supplicant's hand to a stranger for balance? My aunt Lily, sitting on a bench on one of those dirty islands in the middle of Broadway traffic, raising her face for a warming ray of sun? It seems to me I didn't see my relations this often when they were alive.

—

I still had one left. My aunt Rachile was hanging on in California. I went to see her, and we spoke of family matters.

"Your mother," said my aunt Rachile. "I could tell you things about your mother."

"Maybe not today," I said.

It was mean to cut her off like that; grievances had been her life. But my mother had died only a month before and, *really*, she might have had some consideration. But, you know, Rachile had always been histrionic, half-crazed with grievance. I was heartened to see that her center still held. She was a brave girl in her way.

—

In the earliest picture I've ever seen of her, Rachile is in a family group: a passport photo, taken in 1922, in Bucharest. My grandmother and grandfather are there, only in their fifties, staring grimly into the lens. Surrounding them are four of my shockingly young aunts and uncles: Frieda, maybe twenty; Rachile and her twin brother, Joe, eighteen; I see that Berca (who will be called Georgie in America) is about ten, and that his jaw has already been deformed by an untreated infection.

The camera has caught them in extremis: six frightened, bewildered refugees. My refugees (they *are* mine; these pages are their last home) have fled Ukraine and crossed the Romanian border. Running for their lives from famine, pogroms, the Bolshevik revolution, civil war, etc. Running like hell, from history, no less.

Of course at the moment the shutter snaps, they haven't a clue how lucky they are, how much history they will be spared. They are going to America, where my grandfather, clever man, sent his older children before the war; those three—Lily, Oscar, and Bella—are absent from the photo, as is the eldest of the children, Rifka. She's the aunt who stayed behind with her husband and child. Why she stayed, I can't imagine. She'd already been raped during a pogrom. In 1942, history—which, as I was always instructed, consists of vast, inexorable forces, always progressive in tendency— will find her in Odessa, where she and her husband will be killed in the ghetto, along with fifty thousand other Jews. By Romanians, not Germans—if it matters.

—

When Rachile was born, in 1904, she was the sixth child and the fifth girl. Oscar was the only boy. You may recall that he wasn't quite living up to expectations. I need hardly say, then, that Rachile's emergence from the womb was greeted with a groan of . . . *not* joy. But, wait! My bubbe isn't finished; a few minutes later her contractions resume and out comes Joe, the second longed-for son. Poor Rachile. Twice cursed just as her life begins. Two more sons came later, but first impressions are lasting.

———

"What was Bubbe like?" I asked Rachile.

"She was a beast."

Just then I noticed a narrow copper-colored band on Rachile's finger; it left a black trace. Not gold.

"What's that?"

"Your grandmother's wedding ring."

"Can I have it?"

"What do you want it for? It was a miserable marriage."

"Tell more about Bubbe."

"What else do you want? She was beautiful. She was very clean. In summer she always dressed in white. Your grandfather adored her, but she wouldn't sleep with him. She loved her sons. Joe, she loved most of all. Me, she hated. Selfish beast!"

———

That my grandmother favored her sons was a given. In that part of the world, at that time, a son was "an egg with two yolks" (a double irony in the case of these particular twins). But she loved her older daughters. She loved my mother; *that* was gall to Rachile. And also, by the time Rachile came along, her four sisters had carved out their sisterly roles and their places in the family: Lily, the bossy one—*really* bossy; Frieda, the conciliator; Bella, the precocious one. Poor Rachile. How was she going to break into that tight circle? And let's add here that, judging by her temperament in later life, she may have been a hard child to love.

The way it worked in those days was that the girls, when they reached the age of five or six, had to take care of the latest infant. My mother was six when Rachile and Joe were born: *her* turn! But Bella lucked out. (As usual! Rachile would say bitterly.) Shortly before the twins were born, my grandmother's sister, Hannah, arrived from the nearby town of Brailov to help out. Hannah was childless.

"You have too many children," my great-aunt Hannah said to my grandmother. "Give me Bella."

My mother jumped for joy. How she had *dreaded* the prospect of taking care of the new baby. Babies!

Please, please, please! she begged.

So what happened, as Rachile saw it, was that *Bella* got to evade her duty to Rachile, *Bella* got to live in a bigger town, where she could get a better education (she *was* a prize pupil), *Bella* got to live in a household where she got all the love and attention.

And what did Rachile get? *Bupkes.* She got Lily as a caretaker, and Lily was *so* mean to her. She got no education (she never learned to write properly), no affection from her mother—just the opposite. What she did get was all the scut work in the house while the older children went to school; she got to take care of Georgie. And she finally found her role in the family—the scapegoat—and a mode of expression: hysterics.

—

Rachile was no Cinderella who held her tongue. Everything spilled out. Surely, if she rehearsed her wrongs often enough, expressed them with enough feeling, placed enough blame on her persecutors, told enough people, justice would be given her. Anyone could have told her that she was taking exactly the wrong tack, but she couldn't help herself; she really couldn't. She cornered people and railed at them: *my mother! my sisters! Bella this! Lily that!*

—

But I'm getting ahead of myself. It's still 1922, and the ship carrying my refugees is just making port in New York. My father and mother have been married for two years. Oscar and Lily are still single. On the day the ship arrives,

Oscar and Lily are at work, and my mother is putting the final touches on the Bronx apartment where the whole family will live. My father goes to meet the ship. He brings the refugees back to the apartment, and he's smiling. Pretty girls, he says to my mother (in English, so the pretty girls won't understand).

Except for Lily, who was never too much in the looks department, the girls, in youth, are beauties. Rachile is prettiest, after my mother. She's slight, with high cheekbones, dark hair, and hazel eyes. And she is *very* flirtatious, more so than all her sisters put together. Probably she's already given my father the business on the way from the boat to the Bronx, which would account for his smile. But if you happened to be a close observer of human behavior, you might want to be careful of Rachile. Even flirting, she's too intense for comfort; her small, tight half-smile is self-conscious; even as she seduces, and flaunts herself, she watches. And you'd better mind your manners, because the slightest sign of indifference will be quickly interpreted as a direct insult. And then you'd be in for it. Oh! such reproaches, more or less vehemently expressed.

But, remember, we are talking about a very pretty, flirtatious young girl, and soon Rachile meets Victor. At that time, in that world, degrees of separation were no more than two. Victor was Noach's cousin. Noach, I remind you, had first been in love with my mother's best friend, Rose. However, since Rose's heart was already engaged by Albert, Noach asked Rachile for a date. *She* was not one to be satisfied with being second-best.

"Why not Frieda?" Rachile said.

As it turned out this was a very good suggestion. Noach and Frieda lived pretty happily ever after.

With Victor it was another matter. He was handsome, *truly* handsome; not very tall, but a real charmer, with thick, wavy black hair and a way with women: women threw themselves at him. *Women?* Girls. Victor was Rachile's age, barely out of his teens. But girls threw themselves at him. He'd had dozens of girls.

"I love you," said Victor to Rachile in the course of things.

"Liar!" she reproached him.

He wrote her a letter: "I think about you all the time. I can't sleep."

That did it. They got married in 1926.

—

In our house, where a photograph of Lenin hung on the attic wall (I used to think it was my grandfather) and people were always rushing around to Party meetings, anyone with ambition to be holier-than-thou—and Rachile was nothing if not competitive—had her work cut out for her. In 1931, she made a pilgrimage to the Revolution. It happened that she went by herself; Victor, being a milliner—a seasonal trade—was working his season. I'm not sure how many places in the Soviet Union Rachile visited, but I know she was in Odessa. If, in Odessa, she heard some talk about the forced collectivization of the peasantry and its unpleasant consequences, no doubt she dismissed it: You-can't-make-an-omelette-without-breaking-eggs, can you? Didn't the Soviet Union have to modernize, industrialize, overcome centuries of feudalism, and quickly? How else could the five-year plan be realized? And, anyway, how bad could things be? You could still get food in Odessa.

Moreover, a lot of Rachile's attention was taken up with Victor's brother, Misha. (Just how close their friendship became, I can only guess from Rachile's coy references in later years, and from the picture of Misha she showed me; he was even handsomer than Victor, if you can believe it.)

Whatever happened in 1931—it was a short trip—Rachile came home with news of the miraculous Revolution. *Everybody* in the Soviet Union was happy, *everybody* was excited, *everybody* was involved in creating the new Soviet man. Under Stalin's leadership, guided by Marxist-Leninist thought, a new world was being born. She and Victor would have to work very hard, but they *must* be part of this wonderful experiment. Not to mention that the Depression was raging and the final collapse of capitalism was at hand. Therefore, they'd better get on the stick.

So in 1932, off go my aunt and uncle into history's maw, which happens to be a kolkhoz in Ukraine. Of course this was the very moment when Stalin's campaign of terror, his policy of starving this troublesome area to death, was reaching its apogee. This time Rachile noticed.

If my aunt Rachile were alive today, I'd tell her a riddle I recently heard:

Q: *How do we know that Marxism is a theory, not science?*

I don't know, darling. How?

A: *If it were science, they'd have tried it on dogs first.*

I know my aunt; she'd have had the last word: "They did try it on dogs. On cows. On horses. You think the animals had it any better?"

———

Rachile and Victor managed to get out of the Soviet Union about a year later. They came home having seen what they saw and knowing what they knew. Rachile, as you can imagine, was not one to keep her mouth shut. Of course she should have known that you cannot talk to people who have a lock on truth—hadn't she herself been one of them? Of course she would be ignored and reviled! Marx and Lenin,

even forgetting about Stalin, balanced against *Rachile?*
What did *Rachile* know? *She* had no firm political ground-
ing, *she* never studied Marxist theory; *she* was a bourgeoise,
accustomed to the soft life, exaggerating everything as usual,
to make herself important. She was always a troublemaker.
And, anyway, even if there *was* something in it, she was
weak; you had to be like *iron* to be a revolutionary; you can't
make an omelette without breaking a few eggs, isn't that so?

—

Rachile was barely thirty when she and Victor got back to
America. Her sisters and brothers were having children.
Oscar had a little girl; Joe had one too. Lily, that mean
bitch—yes, *bitch*—was barren, which showed there was at
least some justice in the world; Bella had had a miscarriage
but was trying again.

Rachile loved Frieda, hated Lily. Sometimes she loved
Bella, sometimes hated her; not hated, really. Personally, I
think she worshipped her but was kept at a distance. Bella
was Rachile's touchstone. Role model, as they say these days.

"You know, Dotsicle," Rachile said to me once. "Everyone admired your mother. She had a wonderful mind, not
just clever."

—

When Bella gave birth, Rachile was just four months behind
her. Each sister had an adorable little girl. See how many pic-

tures of them were taken by their proud parents! Two tiny girls together in a playpen; on the lap of one father or the other; gazed at adoringly by one mother or the other; on a homemade swing, shamelessly, sweetly naked; barely standing, with their baby arms around each other's shoulders. I think Rachile believed that her child would level the playing field, be her buffer, a liaison to the family; change her status from scapegoat into a woman among women, sister among sisters. The past would fall away.

—

"My sisters ruined my marriage," Rachile told one and all. What did she mean by that? That Victor had affairs with her sisters, serially? I don't think so. Maybe Victor did have affairs, but, according to Rachile, so did she. I think she meant that her sisters took Victor's side.

Miserable creature! Selfish beast! These words followed in her wake like poisonous insects. Victor was heard to remonstrate: "What's the matter with you? None of your sisters got a better husband! They say so, too."

—

But what did I know about all this? I was all warm and cozy in my aunt's love.

"You know, Dotsicle, your mother was always going to meetings. She would leave you with me. They put you in the attic to sleep, and it was so hot up there, you'd cry and cry.

I'd take you out on the roof and walk back and forth with you. I adored you. I loved you so much."

With her own daughter, she didn't do so well. *"Selfish! Miserable creature!"* she screamed at little Vivian.

———

Rachile undertook my education along with her daughter's.

"Girls," said Rachile one day when she picked us up after kindergarten. "Girls, what would you do if a man offers you candy and wants to take you for a ride in his car?"

We looked blank.

"You say *no!* You understand? You tell him, 'My mother said I can't go with you.' "

She left us and went around the corner. A minute later, an old man approached us. "Girls," he said. "Want some candy?"

Vivian and I looked at each other. Candy? She didn't say we couldn't have candy. She said we couldn't have candy *and* go for a ride in a car. I think we already had the candy in our mouths when Rachile came rushing back from her surveillance post around the corner.

"Girls," Rachile said some years later. "What would you do if you were getting undressed and a boy came into the room?"

We were dumb.

"Never be ashamed of your body!" said my aunt Rachile.

"Don't rush to cover yourself up. Be proud." (She herself was very proud. If she happened to be naked when the doorbell rang, she never rushed to cover herself up. *Au contraire.*)

"Girls," Rachile said some years after that. "I have a surprise. I'm taking you to the theater." She took us to see *Darkness at Noon.*

There was a gauntlet thrown down at my mother's feet.

———

As the years went by, Rachile's relations with the rest of the family somehow worsened. Now the focus was money. She got involved in a real estate deal with my father; he promised her big profits. She lost most of the investment and complained bitterly that the *scoundrel* had cheated her (and maybe he did). She claimed that Lily was as mean to Vivian as she had been to Rachile, and that Lily's money was going to Bella's daughter, *nothing* for Vivian. (There was something in that.) She told people that Bella and Lily had conspired to get Oscar's money in their own names, ostensibly so that his first wife couldn't get at it but, really, to keep it for themselves. (I doubt that one.) Even her twin brother, Joe, denied her a loan when she asked for it. Poor Rachile. As happens to bitter, loquacious people, confidants become like hens' teeth.

Rachile and Victor retired to Santa Monica. Victor died there, suddenly, of a heart attack. Soon after that, Rachile moved north, to Oakland, to be close to Vivian. She lived in a retirement home. Her physical health was good, but she was plagued by depression; again and again she said she wanted to die. During those last years I spoke to her by telephone, and saw her a few times. Once, Vivian took her to Florida. I met them there and we all stayed with Bobby, Frieda's daughter.

"You know, Dotsicle," Rachile told me then. "Your mother very much wanted another child after you were born."

"Really?" I said. News to me.

"Yes. But she could never get pregnant again. She used to say to me, 'When we go, Dotsy will be all alone. She'll have no one.' "

———

The very last time I spoke to my aunt Rachile, she was in the hospital.

"How are you, Tante darling?" Did she know who I was?

"Terrible, terrible, Dotsinka."

"Tell me what hurts you."

"That mother I got," she said. "You know the one. I don't feel she gave birth to me. She's like a stranger."

NIGHT FALLS ON

TRANSYLVANIA

—

So. I was grief-stricken. Who would have thought? I'd complained so *bitterly*, and they'd been so *old*; I'd been on a death-watch for *so* long. Grief took me by surprise. Would you believe, for instance, that while standing on line in the supermarket I'd be engulfed by a memory so overwhelming that I'd hear myself moaning aloud?

When something like that happens in a public place, it's best to be nicely dressed.

—

You know, my mother had high hopes of my father's retirement years. Mostly she hoped they would travel. Many of her friends went on tours to China with their husbands, they had adventures at elder hostels, they went to Florida every winter. But Mama couldn't get my father to budge (oh, no! Daddy had business; he had to sit on the porch handing out money to lowlifes); and the older she got the less she wanted to part from him. So you could count the travels of her life on the fingers of one hand: a few trips to Florida to visit her sister Lily; a trip to California to see her cousin Meyer; a bonus visit to St. Louis to see her brother Joe just because the cross-country bus stopped there on the way back from California. And then, in the early seventies, she decided to go home to what was still Soviet Russia. She asked me to come with her.

"Why doesn't Daddy go?" I said, knowing Daddy.

"You know Daddy," she said.

Of *course* I could have gone. Why *didn't* I? And why did I never ask her a simple question?

What was it like where you were born, Mama? Was the countryside beautiful? Did you see mountains? hills? a

river? Was the snow very deep in winter? Did you pick
berries in the spring?

The truth is that even if I'd asked, Mama wouldn't have
been much help. When it came to the natural world, she
tended to be a little high-handed, Marxist even; something
on the order of nature simply being an instrument in the
course of human progress. "It was nice," she might have
said. Or, "It wasn't so nice." Or, "It was the way it was.
Snow? Berries? Sure, we had them."

—

When my mother and father were five years dead, I found
myself in Romania, traveling around Transylvania with my
friend Sylvia. We saw breathtaking things. We saw time im-
memorial. We saw landscapes as beautiful as a fairy tale, all
green, folded hills and silver rivers. We saw people in the poetic postures of backbreaking labor. We were hounded by
Gypsies. We saw women harnessed to plows, and men carrying donkey-burdens on their backs. We saw animals beaten,
and a shepherd kissing his pretty lamb on the mouth. We
saw women spinning yarn by the roadside. We drank instant
coffee mixed with Coca-Cola, because there was no water. We
squatted over foul latrines. We saw children sickened by the
downwind from Chernobyl. We saw the traces of beautiful
ancient cities hideously remade by actually existing Com-

munism. We climbed a mountain with a hundred thousand religious pilgrims. We saw Jews from America trying to find traces of families lost in Romania's Holocaust. We saw the Museum of Totalitarianism, and outside, we met an old man who had spent forty-one years in Siberia. We were housed and fed by virtual strangers.

On an evening in early June, we drove to see friends of Sylvia's at their dacha, just outside a city called Miercurea-Ciuc. A rutted dirt road led to a few little houses, each with its own garden, clustered at the bottom of a high green hill. We made toasts and drank schnapps. We went to the house next door, where our host's sister lived with her family, drank more schnapps, made more toasts. Stories were told in Hungarian. We laughed. I told stories in English. We laughed. We ate little meatballs and bread with mustard, and drank some more. A sudden rainstorm rolled over the hill. When it had passed we climbed the hill to the summit, up to rolling meadows covered with wildflowers.

The evening glowed with the clear, golden light of summer twilight after rain. The sound of cowbells broke the stillness, and a procession of a hundred cows majestically crested the hill. Two dogs dashed in ecstatic circles. The thirteen-year-old daughter of the family ran ahead, perfectly, heartbreakingly beautiful in this moment of her life.

It had been dusk, only a few nights before, when I stood at the edge of the Tisza River looking across at Ukraine. I wasn't quite there, but I was as close as I was ever going to get. And now, in this odd and wracked corner of the world, on this hill, in the midst of this family I had never seen before and never would again, grief slipped away. I felt happy as the day is long. Maybe it was the schnapps. Night fell.

STRANGERS IN
THE HOUSE

———

*I've made a list of questions
to which I no longer expect answers,
since it's either too early for them,
or I won't have time to understand.*

—Wisława Szymborska

The Making of Me

I ran into Jack Hoffman on the street. I hadn't seen him in ages.

We said "How are you?" and "What's new?"

"Did you hear?" he said. "Victor's dead. Heart attack. Five years ago."

"Really?" I said.

"Yes," he said. "Really."

"Dr. Nielsen?" I said the first time I went to his office.

He nodded. He never argued with that form of address.

This was Victor Nielsen, not any sort of doctor; a former opera singer (Danish). Those were the days when anyone could hang out a shingle as a "lay" analyst.

You might expect a Dane to be tall and blond. Not so Victor. He was about fifty then, not in the least handsome, short and stocky, with a fleshy face. But he had a large head, thick gray hair, and he looked bigger sitting down. Sitting down was a major part of his job. Also he had very blue eyes; and his low, well-trained, charmingly accented voice, a beautiful voice, which gave him great authority; and in the end you had to say that, all in all, he was an attractive man.

His office was somewhere on the Upper West Side, Eighty-sixth Street, I think, just a few doors in from Broadway. It was a large room, bright, uncurtained, just above street level. Standing, you had a perfect view of the street life below; sitting, you saw the heads of people walking past the windows. I sat across the desk from Victor. ("Call me Victor," he said, waving away any need for the spurious title.) I had expected a leather couch, but his office contained only the desk, a couple of chairs, a Marimekko sort of rug, and a daybed with a rough cotton throw, drab blue, as I remember. In due course, I thought, I would be invited to lie down.

Why was I there? Hindsight shows me that I was just ahead of the sea change. Only a few years later, a nineteen-year-old girl—confused, moody, depressed, reluctantly promiscuous—would be engulfed by a culture and a cause—drugs, casual sex, communes, Vietnam; would know what clothes to wear—vintage dresses, army castoffs, jeans, T-shirts; would know how to do her hair—parted in the middle, flowing down her back; and would know what music belonged to her—Dylan, Baez, etc. As it was, I wore the hateful garter belts and stockings of my time, straight woolen skirts and shirtwaist dresses; set my hair every night to appear as a shoulder-length pageboy in the morning; listened to Frank Sinatra and Vaughn Monroe, who certainly weren't bad but weren't mine.

My mother was at her wits' end. She consulted her cousin Sylvia, the social worker.

"I can't deal with her," my mother said. "She leaves school, she stays out all night, she won't tell me where she goes, she moves out of the house, she moves back in, she can't keep a job, she won't talk to me."

Sylvia, being a social worker, knew what to do. "Send her to an analyst," she said. "I know someone."

So now I was sitting across the desk from my analyst, and what did he say to me?

"I'm going to make a real little woman out of you."

Once a week, over a couple of years, I saw Victor Nielsen. Apart from that promise, which he often repeated, I can't remember another word of what passed between us. No doubt I talked about my mother, my father, and how they had ruined my life. At the time, I happened to be lovesick for a man who would marry me two years later; in the meantime, he had dumped me, and I was sleeping with almost anyone who asked. Each time I told Victor about one of these incidents, he said, "You have the makings of a real little woman."

Who was right about this: Victor? Or my father, who had taken to calling me a prostitute?

Well of course I was not a prostitute, although I could see where he might get that idea. If he had known about it, for instance, my father could have said that I once did it for a dime. I was visiting San Francisco, and a guy whose name I no longer remember had kindly taken me to see the sights. We spent a long day together, and then a long evening. After dinner he suggested we spend the night together. I was staying across the Bay, in Berkeley, with my cousin Vivian. It was late, it was raining, I was tired. I didn't particularly like this guy, and furthermore, I had my period. I thought about this. And then I thought about waiting for the bus, which ran infrequently at that hour, about the long bus ride to Berkeley, and about the walk through the rain to my cousin's house. The dime was the bus fare.

I had once briefly shared an apartment with a girl who was desperate to lose her virginity. She was very strange. The things that happened to me happened to girls all the time. And it was always easier to say yes. "No" was impolite. "No" would be taken personally.

"Why not?" the guy would say incredulously. "Don't you like me?" That was a possibility so far out of the question, it had never entered his mind.

Or he might get mean: "Are you frigid?"

Such a foolish girl! So acquiescent to the imperious male. So careful of his pride. One night I let such a guy, prideful, imperious, take me to bed. He was not only married, he was impotent, and he wanted to keep trying again and again. It was extremely unpleasant. Finally, I said, "No, really, no more." I was very nice. I didn't mention that I was sore and exhausted and repelled. I didn't mention that he didn't have the wherewithal. I politely said, "Listen, I know you're married; I don't like one-night stands."

He turned vicious. "You better get used to one-night stands," he said, "because that's all you're ever going to have."

You'd think that Victor might have helped me out with these situations.

After a couple of years, Bob and I got married, and I didn't see Victor again until Bob and I separated three years later. By that time I had a boyfriend named Jack. (Yes, that Jack; the Jack who would tell me that Victor had died.) And here's where the story gets interesting.

Jack had once been married to a girl named Sheila. Sheila was not happy in the marriage. She went to see an analyst. Guess who? Victor! And guess who Sheila was now married to? Victor! They had a little baby.

"Really?" I said.

By the way, I said to Victor, "Isn't this situation—you, me, Jack, Sheila, all of us involved in one way and another—isn't it, well, a problem for you, professionally speaking?"

"No problem," Victor said. "You'll like Sheila. She was a confused little girl when she first came to see me, but now she's a real little woman." He added, "You and Jack, you come and spend a weekend with us."

Jack and I spent several weekends with Victor and Sheila. We all became good friends. Of course, I saw more of Victor than that, since he was still my analyst.

One day I told Victor I was tired of Jack.

"Ah," Victor said.

And it seemed that due course had arrived.

Victor took my hand and led me to the daybed with the blue cotton cover. I lay down. In that position I could no longer see people walking by on the street. All I could see was Victor's fleshy face looming over me. He murmured in my ear: "You see? You're a real little woman now."

Whoever You Were

I was living up on Ninety-ninth and Broadway, remember? In that studio on the fifteenth floor? Only one window, the kitchen hidden in a closet like a Murphy bed. I liked that apartment. No surprises, no one lurking in another room.

Sure, you remember that place. You lurked across the street most of that cold winter, sometimes late into the night, watching the entrance, waiting to catch the man I preferred to you.

How in God's name did you think you'd ever spot him, anyway? Do you know how many apartments there were in that building? Sixty, seventy apartments, maybe. Men coming and going all the time. Men who lived in that building, one of whom, I'll tell you now, was my lover. Jack. Jack, who lived one flight above me. It was a joke.

No, no, not a joke. I only made jokes because I was appalled. What had I done? And Bob, dear Bob, sweet Bob, you were out of control, you were over the edge. Crazy Bob. Remember the

New Year's Eve after I left? You rang my doorbell. Jack was with me. I was afraid to let you in, I was afraid not to. I said, "This is Jack, my upstairs neighbor." At last you had caught me with a man, and you didn't put two and two together. Why not? Of course, Jack was just this really short guy, not attractive, not even to me, but still, you must have wanted not to know. If you'd known, you'd have had to hit him with those brass knuckles you were carrying around. Brass knuckles! Where the hell did you get brass knuckles?

Jack left, and then we were alone. I asked you to leave too, but you wouldn't. You were acting so nice and friendly, smiling, it was all wrong, you scared me, Bob. I went into the bathroom and locked the door. I stayed there until you finally gave up and I heard the door close behind you. Only later did I realize you'd gotten what you came for. You found my address book. You wrote down the telephone number of every man listed (there were only three or four possible candidates, weren't there? The others were my therapist, my cousins, our friends), and you called each of them. Somehow you got a couple of them to agree to meet you, and you bought them a drink. They told me you had smiled at them in what you thought was the friendliest way, and you demanded that each one admit he was the guy. They denied it. Who wouldn't deny it, you with your menacing smile and your right pocket bulging with brass knuckles? And then you went to see my therapist, and he told my mother, and then she started sending me clippings from the *Daily Mirror*: HUS-BAND KILLS ESTRANGED WIFE! HUSBAND KILLS LOVER OF ESTRANGED WIFE, ESTRANGED WIFE AND SELF!

What had I done? I wasn't used to being so effective. And I have to say, it was very exciting, the drama of it all.

• • •

Remember Beth Kelly? Wasn't she beautiful? So blond and delicate. Oh my God, so many years have passed I wouldn't know her if she sat down next to me. (Would I know you now? Or you me, as far as that goes?) Beth wanted to be a movie star, she could have been a movie star, but I guess she never made it. If not for Beth, I might never have left you.

When Beth came home from summer stock that fall, she was pregnant. You knew that, didn't you? Two months pregnant. It could have been Larry's baby: he'd gone to visit her once or twice that summer. She could have said it was Larry's.

We were all living in the West Village then, practically in the same house; you and I separated by one brownstone wall from Larry and Beth. I can see those houses as clearly as if we still lived there. I still marvel at the rent—the whole house, four floors, for $250, heat included. I remember all the places we lived and how we furnished them. I remember that awful black platform couch we bought at the Door Store, and the crewel wing chair I bought secondhand from an ad in *The Village Voice*. (It was $25, and I felt so smug because Harold and Joan had paid $350 at Macy's for one exactly like it.)

The day after Beth got home, she came over to see me. It was in early September, such a hot day. I was in the kitchen with the door to the backyard wide open. I was glad to see her; I'd missed her. She looked a little pale, though, and I said something like, Gee, Beth, you look tired, are you okay? And she said, No, I'm pregnant. I said, Really! She just looked at me. So then I said, Do you want it? And she said, No. It's not Larry's. I'm not having it. I'm getting a divorce.

Adultery. Abortion. Divorce. I can't tell you how that constellation hit me. Honestly, I think I only knew those words from novels. Beth and Larry were our friends, they'd gotten married a few weeks before we did, they had dinner with us almost every other night, they went to the movies with us, we sat talking at Pete's Tavern for hours. We were a foursome. If those huge words had to do with them, what about us? What about me? Was I allowed? Not that I had committed Adultery. Not yet. Not that I was Pregnant. Not yet.

We weren't doing well, you knew that. Two years into marriage, and sex was such a sometime thing. That was my doing. Remember the time you'd been away in Chicago for a week? When you came home, I didn't want to. And you said, "You know, I had plenty of chances in Chicago, but I wanted you."

Yes. I knew how attractive you could be to women. Hadn't I been one of them myself? It seemed like only yesterday I had wanted you, and all the time; I'd been desperate to marry you for three years, miserable while you went out with this one and that one—Della, Phyllis, Alice, Ruth . . . And then you capitulated. Entirely, with your whole heart you gave yourself to me, I became the one who was halfhearted. So I had what I had wanted, and I was unhappy all the time.

I'm remembering something else: a few weeks after you got home from Chicago, we went out to dinner at one of those French restaurants on Fifty-fifth or Fifty-sixth Street; Steak Frites, I think it was, there used to be so many of those cheap and decent little French restaurants then. Did we sit silently over our meal? Did we speak cold monosyllables? At one point you got up from the table, maybe you went to the bathroom or to make a phone call. The owner of the café came over to me. She said, "Did you know the gentleman sitting alone at that table?" She pointed. I turned. The table behind us was empty. I said, "No, I didn't notice him." She handed me an envelope. She said, "The gentleman was by himself, he said it was his birthday, and he wanted you to have this." There was nothing written on the envelope, there was no note inside, only a ten-dollar bill. Ten dollars wasn't a lot of money even in those days. And this is what I imagined: the man, middle-aged (he was probably younger than we are today), had watched us at our silent dinner. What did he see? A thin young girl with short dark hair, silent, sad; a redheaded man, a little older, frustrated and angry because the girl was so sullen. The observing man wanted to tell the girl something. That she was pretty? That she reminded him of someone in his past? That things would get better for her, maybe? The French restaurant, the young unhappy couple, the older man eating his lonely birthday dinner in a cheap restaurant, telling himself our story. Romantic, wasn't it?

Joan. Now, Joan was happy. She was pregnant and happy, she and Harold were happy. I said, "Joan, I'm so unhappy, what should I do?" She said, "Stop nagging him. Bob's great. Maybe he's a little erratic, but that's the way he is. He's brilliant."

Yes, it's true: you were erratic, brilliant, flying one minute, crashing the next, full of grandiose plans I didn't understand, drinking too much, eating too much. And then somebody would put a spoke in your wheel at work, or I'd say, "Bob, you're crazy, you can't just build a hydrogen balloon . . . whatever!"

You know, the strange thing is that I can hear you, your beautiful lilting tenor, singing one of those corny Irish ballads you used to sing to me . . . *"She was lovely and fair as the first*

rose of summer / But it was not her beauty alone that won me /
Oh no, t'was the truth in her eyes ever shining / That made me
love Mary, the Rose of Tralee . . ." But I can't bring back the
sound of your voice when you spoke to me.

No, I wouldn't go with you in any hydrogen balloon, but
I did something just as dangerous. I went on the *Athlone* with
you. I remember so many things about that boat: it was twenty-
three feet long, it had a steel hull, it had been built in Holland, it
was a sloop—a mainsail, a jib, ropes that rubbed my fingers raw,
a minuscule cabin with two bunks, each wide enough to sleep a
snake. I got on board and let you sail me from Gravesend Bay,
up the East River, and all the way to Martha's Vineyard, with no
motor except a three-horsepower outboard that conked out in
the Narrows.

You didn't know a thing about sailing, did you, except
what you taught yourself from a book. That's where you were so
brilliant. You could teach yourself anything, the most complicated technical things, from a book. Remember when you told
me that boats under sail always have the right of way? If you
knew so much, why did we nearly drown when that cruise ship
didn't change course in New York Harbor?

Three long weeks on the tiny boat, sometimes heeled so far
over that the mainsail skimmed the water; tacking back and
forth, back and forth across the Sound; becalmed in fog for a
day and night; on a roller coaster of stormy seas; soaking-wet
bunks; eating canned corned beef hash morning, noon, and
night. (Oh, sometimes Dinty Moore beef stew.) I wanted to
scream! But we had some moments, didn't we? Like that perfect
evening, the time of day when the wind dies and the sea goes
flat. We were tied up in a harbor, down in the cabin heating up

hash over the Sterno stove, when there was a bump against the boat. We climbed up on deck. A school of porpoises was circling the boat, playing with it, playing with us, jumping out of the water, bumping us, circling round and round. They stayed with us for almost an hour as the sun went down, they were close enough to touch, and I did, I reached down and petted one as he swam by. He seemed to jump for joy. That was a glory, wasn't it?

And that sun-struck day in open ocean, out of sight of land, zipping right along on a following wind. On impulse I took off my clothes, jumped into the water . . . and surfaced all alone in the middle of the ocean, the *Athlone* sailing on until it was just a speck, almost to the horizon. It took such a long, long time for you to head into the wind, turn the boat around, tack, tack, tack back for me, but you did it, I knew you could, I treaded water and waited for you.

It was Helen who brought me to 85 Perry Street that first night. Maybe you don't remember Helen—my friend from Hunter, Jerry's girlfriend for a little while. She passed through Perry Street pretty quickly, she passed through my life pretty quickly too. But she brought me to that house, and what a house it was, two floors of it, wide-plank floorboards, and four older guys (in your late twenties to our eighteen, a lifetime older) living in what seemed like a perpetual party, girlfriends coming and going—a wonder of a place to a girl from Washington Heights, how I wanted to be one of those girlfriends.

I was brought for you that night. But oh no; at the last minute Della had to push her way in. "A party!" said Della. "Can I come?" Helen looked at me. I said okay. What else could I say? I would have said no if Della hadn't been so pretty; I had my pride. You remember Della: tall, blond, a knockout. You took her home that night.

Oh, that was a cruel blow! Because I had already planned my life around you. Yes, the minute I saw you, I knew that you would mean the world to me. Just that. The world. My Open Sesame.

Della wouldn't last long. You were too rough a diamond for Della, she thought too well of herself, she thought she was entitled to more polish, better social credentials. But for me, you were more than good enough, whoever you were.

I wrote to you last year. Did you get my letter? Did you not remember who I was? Or did you just decide you didn't want to answer? Were you too medicated to answer? Yes, I know you're medicated, that you've been in the hospital. Depression, Harold told me; he says you talk very slowly. That must be the medication. Do you know that Joan died?

Harold is the only one I still know from our time together. Helen, Beth, Della—they all disappeared from my life. I wanted to tell you that I remember everything that happened to us. All the big things—love, marriage, abortion, adultery, divorce—happened to us, happened first to us. I know that you married again, that you have two children, grown now, that you sit quietly all day with a book on your lap, reading, or maybe just staring at the page.

Another thing I wanted to mention. About the cold winter when you still lived on Perry Street, and you were going out with Ruth, Alice, Della, Phyllis, whoever. And I was crazy with love for you and lurked across from your house late into the night, waiting to see you with the girl you preferred to me.

What You See Is What You Get

By 1970 I had lived in Brooklyn Heights for five or six years, and during the last couple of years I was on my own. Every morning I rode the subway under the river to my job at a magazine in the city; every evening I came back to that peaceful, leafy enclave. So peaceful. So leafy.

Sometimes, for a change of scene, I'd walk the length of the Promenade to the north end, and down the steep hill that led to the gritty flats on the river. If not for some ancient faces peering from tenement windows—relics of the once-thriving waterfront—you would have thought that the streets under the Brooklyn Bridge were deserted. The buildings fronting the river looked like a movie set waiting for action. Among the boarded-up shops was one café still in business, although it was empty the day I happened to take a picture of it.

I look at that photograph now, and it takes me back to a lonely time: my twenties were recent history, my marriage was behind me, my Nikon was in my hand, and I was searching for a way into the picture. I'm reminded that the day was windy, the air was fresh, a hard bright light glanced off the choppy river. And here is the picture I took: a plate-glass window with RESTAURANT in gilt, half chipped off. On the far side of the window, you can see the café in wait: metal-ringed Formica tables set with napkin holders, glass sugar dispensers, and salt and pepper shakers, their metal tops gleaming in the sun. And there, in the reflection of the window, is my shadow, the light-struck river, and the Manhattan skyline behind, like a city dreamed of. A block or two away, out of camera range, is the house where Norman Peterson lived.

Norman Peterson had found a dilapidated two-room building to hold his precarious life. Upstairs he slept on a cot and made his strange metal sculptures; the dark downstairs room was the kitchen. When you got to know him, you felt that those rooms, in the deep shadow of the soaring span of the bridge, enveloped by the constant hum of interborough traffic, smelling of the gas station next door, were his natural home.

Norman came from Seattle. His uncle was a commercial fisherman. As a boy, Norman had worked the boats. He talked sometimes about winter expeditions up Puget Sound and on to the coast of Alaska, the temperature so low that salt spray froze his eyes shut. He got away from that life by joining the army. After that, on the GI Bill, he took a course in welding, thinking it would be a useful trade to keep him on land. Then something unsuspected happened. He began to make sculptures from the metal he welded. He was an artist! He knew it! And where in the world did that ever come from, a boy who'd never known an artist, seen an art book, much less been to a museum? A boy from as deep into the working class as you could get.

And then he really got out. He went to live the artist's life on an Aegean island—Hydra—where a colony of artists had migrated. He told me who they were, but the only one I remember is Leonard Cohen. It was a paradise: sunshine every day, work in the morning, swimming in the afternoon, dinners that went on into the small hours, Leonard Cohen singing his songs, vast quantities of vile wine and willing women.

Hydra was Norman's moment: he'd found his way into a life. But then Leonard Cohen left the island ("So long, Marianne . . ."), and the colony disintegrated. Where else do artists congregate? Norman came to my cold, costly city, where no gallery was interested in his work and the circles of artists were closed to him. He went on working, but no one saw his work, and certainly no one bought his work. He found an old panel truck and made a living as a moving man.

When I met Norman, he was in his late thirties, though you might easily have guessed forties. He had a truck driver's build: big and lumbering, strong, with a beer belly. He rolled his own cigarettes. He usually wore a hat, a Greek fisherman's cap in winter, a straw hat tilted against the sun in summer. I liked his looks—his height, his physical strength, his black hair and mustache, his clear gray eyes. But I was put off too: he was wary, mostly silent, gruff when he spoke. Conversation was definitely not his sport.

I was of two minds about Norman. Sometimes I thought of him as an innocent fool, without vanity or self-consciousness, without a clue as to how much of a misfit he was. His social skills were close to nil, which carried over to the arts of flirtation and flattery. He had no idea how to make use of himself with women—with urban women, anyway; uptown girls, he called them, girls like me. (I suspect he was accustomed to more direct transactions with women.) But I had other moods when I saw him as the gold standard, a simon-pure original, aware of it, and on guard against assaults to his integrity.

In practical terms, of course, the distinction didn't matter. He was, he always would be, elusive, isolated, an oddball. Yes, I was interested, but I knew that what I saw was what I'd get. I never lost my heart. So when the lease on my apartment ran out and Norman said, "Live with me," I laughed. That was mean. But really, did he think my prospects were so dim that I would make my life with a de facto hermit in his dank dark hovel?

Now Wendy Samson, she had a way with her.

"Oh hi! I'm so glad to meet you!" she would say on meeting someone new. "I loved your piece about . . ." and Wendy would turn to a person nearby and tell that person that you were a brilliant writer, painter, poet . . . whatever it was you happened to profess. Then she would inform you that this other person was also brilliant at something or other. Simply being introduced to Wendy Samson brought membership in a coterie of brilliant people, who seemed to be the only sort of people Wendy knew. I was quite taken with her.

Wendy and I had recently become colleagues. We were staff writers at a famous magazine for young women, which meant that we got a salary for which we owed the magazine a certain number of articles a year. We didn't have to go into the office very often, and we could also write for other publications. It was a terrific job. A sort of subsidized freelance career.

I wasn't able to match Wendy's flattery, as I hadn't yet read anything she'd written. But I'd heard her spoken of in admiring terms as a rising star of journalism (celebrity profiles, reports from the cultural front). Wendy had the looks for media stardom. She was about thirty then, tall, leggy, slender, a little stooped, as tall girls often were in those days. But her thick black hair cascaded down her back. She wore aviator glasses in the style made ubiquitous—required, even—by Gloria Steinem, who was her hero (role model, as we used to say) and who also happened to wear her hair the same way. And, as pretty young women with good legs did, as Gloria Steinem did, Wendy dressed in miniskirts. She was filled with nervous energy: her foot jiggled, she leaned in close, her speech was rushed, confiding, avid.

Although I hadn't read Wendy's pieces, I had read about her in an interview in which Wendy and her husband conversed on the subject of the "two-career marriage." Her husband was, naturally, a brilliant academic; Wendy, brilliant in her own way, had chosen a career in the popular prints. She and her husband, by compromising when necessary, by giving each other the gift of loving respect and maneuvering room, had made their marriage into a triumphant model of modern relations between the sexes. A photograph accompanied the article: beautiful Wendy holding hands with her very handsome husband. They were an enviable couple. So when I mentioned to Wendy that I was looking for an apartment and she suggested that I share hers, well, you can imagine my surprise.

The husband had fled. Another woman. Wendy was shocked, devastated, brave. I went to inspect the former marital home. It was one of those vast, rambling apartments on the

Upper West Side. There was a huge foyer, a large living room, a dining room, a bedroom wing with two bedrooms, each with a bath, and somewhere in the dim recesses, a maid's room and a kitchen. The main rooms were heavily furnished with vaguely Spanish-style furniture, large pieces that seemed not so much chosen as too much trouble to remove.

I looked around. The apartment could be split down the middle: a bedroom for me, the dining room turned into my living room; we'd share the kitchen. I had a few reservations. I was used to living on my own, and for the most part, I liked it. I didn't have such a good history of living with people— roommates in the distant past, husbands more recently. But I knew something about solitude: it could easily become too much of a good thing.

"Yes, okay," I said to Wendy. "Let's try it."

Norman helped me pack my belongings into his panel truck. He moved me in late one night and stayed until morning. For Norman, Wendy varied her formula: "Oh, he's so interesting, isn't he?" she said.

I didn't see as much of Norman Peterson after that. He came uptown from time to time, usually unannounced. One evening he brought me a sculpture. It looked like a heart—a real heart, I mean, an anatomical heart, with the aorta attached—or maybe like a heavy-bottomed seabird with a narrow head. He said he was starting to do ceramics again, and that he was thinking about making lamps.

"Sell them to those designers," he said. "Make some money."

"Good idea," I said.

"How are you doing?" he asked. "Like living here?"

Did I like living there?

By then I'd been living at Wendy's for about six months, and it was beginning to seem like the central fact of my life. In theory we shared the apartment: we split the rent, we each had a set of rooms, separate lives. Yes, I could close my door, do my work, see friends. But by some alchemy, Wendy filled all the space. I never knew quite how she did it. She was like a black hole: all matter, all energy that entered her gravitational field, was sucked in. Late at night (she stayed up very late), late in the morning (she got up very late), I heard her shuffling footsteps going past my closed door. I felt reproach in her every step. Because what was I doing when my door was closed?

I wasn't helping Wendy!

Wendy was afflicted. Naturally. Her husband had chosen another. Actually, it was something more material than Wendy's negative energy that took up so much room. Many days and many nights, three or four of her friends were summoned to console her. Occasionally, her daytime phone invitations—"Do you want to go for a walk in the park?"—or the late-evening calls—"Come over and let's talk"—failed to produce anybody, and Wendy found herself alone. How she hated being alone! When that happened, she came to my room, her bathrobe scruffy, her hair lank, advertising depression. She sat on the edge of my bed and talked and talked. She rehearsed the years of her marriage, the unforgivable betrayal that she had done nothing to deserve (indeed, she had been the most generous and loving of wives). I listened. At first I was sympathetic. I'd been there.

But with each retelling of the story, a little more information slipped out. Perhaps Wendy hadn't been such a loving wife after all. Perhaps, she said (with what I would call a snicker), she had become bored with marital sex and had had a few affairs with the celebrity subjects of her interviews.

"Well. But Wendy. If you were having sex with everybody except your husband . . ."

Wendy was affronted: "But he didn't know that," she wailed.

How could I be so insensitive?

And did I say that three or four of Wendy's friends would appear almost daily? Seven or eight of her friends. Old school friends, strangers passing through town who'd gotten Wendy's name from some acquaintance, it made no matter. They slept in the maid's room, they slept on the couches, they stayed for days, sometimes weeks. And what did they do in her apartment, in my apartment? They helped Wendy.

All night long—because Wendy liked nothing more than to be awake in the small hours, talking about her crisis—they consoled her, they gossiped with her, some slept with her. And, being brilliant, each and every one, they helped her write her pieces. They went over her notes, they helped her organize them, they showed her where the narrative was, they found her lead, they worked out the sentences. Now that just drove me up the wall.

Did I like living there?

I went to Brooklyn to see Norman's lamps. I was astonished. I was used to his weird, abstract, distinctly unbeautiful pieces. These were gorgeous. Steel, glowing like old pewter, made sweeping arcs through the air. They were more than sculptural, they were sculptures. Beautiful.

"They're beautiful," I said. "Anybody would want them. I want one. There's one problem."

"What?"

"It's not a lamp if there's hardly any light."

Norman considered. Would a lamp that actually illuminated ruin his artistic intent?

"I don't know," he said.

He was so annoying. Didn't he want to sell them? Didn't he want some worldly reward?

Norman and I were not lovers anymore, but he kept in touch. He kept in touch more than I liked. He hoped. Had the words been available to him, I think he would have said he loved me. At any rate, he aspired to me.

I was seriously thinking about moving. It was such a drag to move. Looking for another place, packing up everything, unpacking, organizing stuff, my work interrupted for weeks. But you can imagine: my life was a nightmare. Even if you don't want to go to the party, you want to be asked to the party. I knew that I had brought it all on myself. My disdain for Wendy's life—what would in later years be called her "lifestyle"—was palpable.

Many nights I felt imprisoned in my room. I was reluctant even to walk through the crowd to go to the kitchen. One night, outside my door, the Hog Farm had gathered. Remember the Hog Farm? I had not bargained for this, for life in a dorm, life at summer camp. And just as there is a pariah at every summer camp, I was the outcast here, the wet blanket, the sourpuss, the person consumed with envy—at Wendy's success: her social and professional success (yes, many famous men, all of them brilliant, naturally, sought her out to sexually console her; once consolation had taken place, they were pressed into helping Wendy with her work—into doing her work). Well, no, I never had asked anyone for help, but why was no one offering to console me? To help me? Oh, and did I mention that Wendy's brother was now living in the apartment full-time, another tenant without a by-your-leave? Golly, I was bitter.

I took a week off and went to Monhegan Island, where my friend Kitty was staying. I must have mentioned it to Norman, because the day after I got to the island, I ran into him toiling up the hill from the ferry, wearing his straw summer hat tilted against the sun. He was in good spirits. People had liked his lamps. Galleries were dubious, but a high-end shop had taken a few on consignment. "Yeah," he said, "I made the light brighter."

He asked me where I was staying. "Do you have your own room?"

I had my own room at the hotel. Yes, he could stay with me. It was summer, I was on vacation, he had come all this way for me. Why not? "But Norman," I said, "this doesn't change anything." Norman's lovemaking had never been persuasive enough to change anything.

When I got back to the city, I told Wendy that I'd be moving out as soon as I found a place.

"Not until October," she said. "I need to find another roommate."

"You have another roommate," I said. "Your brother lives

here. And, from night to night, so do any number of other people. Rosemary, Derek, Peter, Mary, the Hog Farm . . . I could go on."

"You know," she said, "your friend Kitty stayed here one night, and you didn't even ask me."

She had me there.

I found a place at the end of July. A loft downtown, on the Bowery. I packed my clothes, my papers, my books. Everything was in cartons. I came home one afternoon to find Wendy's brother unpacking my book cartons.

"What are you doing?"

"Wendy says you took her *New York Times Cookbook*."

"It's my *New York Times Cookbook*," I said. And how dare you?

A food fight. Exactly the right parting note.

I got out of there. I felt so light I was floating, dancing on air.

Things weren't panning out for Norman. One of his lamps had sold, but the others were just sitting in the shop and soon were returned to him. He'd had another idea: he was making furniture out of plumbing materials. Beds, couches, chairs, all from copper pipes and brass fittings. I thought they were wonderful. He gave me a love seat for my new loft. Again shops had taken some pieces on consignment, but time passed, and they didn't sell.

I hadn't seen Norman for a couple of months when he showed up at my loft one day. "I gave up my place," he said. "I'm going back to Hydra." But first he was going to visit his mother out west. "Can I stay here until I leave?"

He was very depressed. He had no place to live. So I said okay, but just for a few days. He sat on my new love seat all day long, drinking, smoking, barely speaking. He was ruining my new sense of freedom. He was a downer. After three days I said he had to go, and he did. He disappeared from my life.

If I thought of Norman at all in the next months, I thought of him on Hydra. But about five months after he left, I got a letter postmarked Seattle. It wasn't from Norman, it was a notice from a mortuary. One of those printed "In Remembrance" cards.

I learned that Norman had been born on February 3, 1934. That he had died on November 12, 1978. That the service had been held at a Presbyterian chapel in Seattle three days later, and that the burial had been courtesy of the United States Army. Inside the printed mortuary notice was a handwritten note:

> Dorothy, it is so hard for me to write the sad news. Norman left a note asking me to notify his friends.
>
> He was with us 4 weeks. He had spent a few months at VA hospital in Maine. He said they had helped him.
>
> He was so depressed, & was leaving to go back on late plane on 12th. In the night his tragedy occurred.
>
> He left a long note saying his work was finished & could foresee no future. As yet I have not been able to accept it and am heartbroken . . .
>
> His mother . . .

So Norman had never gotten to Hydra. He'd had a ticket on a plane to New York. I wondered where he had been planning to stay, I wondered if he had been planning to call me for a place to stay. I wondered if he'd wondered what I would say. I wondered what he'd been thinking on the night of November 12, when he changed his mind.

A year or so later, I was startled to see furniture made of copper tubing and brass fittings in a high-end designer shop. I went in.

"These are very beautiful," I said. "Who made them?"

The shopkeeper named someone I had never heard of. He said that the furniture had been made from original designs by an artist. "Which artist?" I asked. He didn't know. I asked the prices: $2,000 for a double bedstead, $1,000 for a glass-topped coffee table. So. Norman's ideas had been good enough to rip off. Considering everything, I think he would have been glad to know that.

Rarely do I see Wendy's byline these days. When I come across it, I read her pieces with great interest; pleasure, in fact, since it doesn't seem to me that she's getting much help these days. Once in a blue moon, I run into Wendy herself. The last time we met was in a bookshop. She was very friendly.

"That was a brilliant piece you wrote about . . ." she said. "Why don't you call me? We can go for a walk in the park."

As we happened to be standing next to the cookbook section it occurred to me to mention that I'd solved the mystery of her missing *New York Times Cookbook*. Probably she hadn't had much occasion to refer to it during the two years I lived in her apartment. I had since learned that her copy had gone with the fleeing husband.

I hardly remember those days.

Mystery Woman Ruled Dead;
Lost Since Break with Reds

> *A bizarre international mystery, with political under-*
> *themes, zig-zagging from Berlin to Moscow, ended its*
> *final chapter on an unsolved note yesterday as Juliet*
> *Stuart Poyntz, former American Communist leader, [was*
> *declared] legally dead.*
>
> *—New York Daily Mirror,*
> FEBRUARY 13, 1944

On a long-ago afternoon I came home from school to find my mother sitting at the kitchen table. She was reading a newspaper. It wasn't one of the newspapers she usually read. In our house we read the *New York Post;* also *PM.* And *The Daily Worker.* I was intrigued, so I read over my mother's shoulder.

Who was she, this Juliet Poyntz? What was this mystery? Surely I asked my mother these questions.

And surely my mother would have said: "No one you knew, darling; it's not important." No one ever told me anything.

But over the years I sometimes recalled the feeling of consternation in our house that day—a flurry of telephone calls, low-pitched conversations. And when the time came, when I was ready to take an interest in the world that had so absorbed my family, I looked into the matter.

Let me begin here.

On May 28, 1936, less than a year before Juliet Stuart Poyntz disappeared, a woman, later described as young, attractive, blond, and Slavic-looking, went to the ticket counter at Chicago's Union Station. She told the ticket agent that her name was Mary Delmar, and in that name she bought a ticket for a lower berth to New York.

Certain things that followed from the purchase of that ticket are documented, others I can only surmise. I know, for instance, that Mary Delmar boarded the train, and that once she was aboard, she put on a pair of pajamas. I know that they were red pajamas. I assume that Mary Delmar, clad in her red pajamas, then lay down on her berth. And, presumably, as the wheels chugged and the whistle blew and the lights of towns flashed by, troubled thoughts kept Mary awake. Somewhere along the line, she made a decision, and when the train stopped to take on coal at Denholm, Pennsylvania, Mary Delmar, still wearing her red pajamas, jumped off. She left her suitcase behind and carried only two small things: a silver pocketknife with a man's name crudely scratched on it, and a photograph of a little boy.

Mary walked, ran, or stumbled some unspecified distance from the railroad tracks. At last she stopped, exhausted, and fell asleep in a clump of bushes at the edge of a horse pasture. At five o'clock on the morning of May 29, she was discovered by a local farmhand. He took her to the house of his employers, a family named Dolan, who gave Mary shelter.

For almost two weeks Mary remained with the Dolans. They may have been glad to have an extra hand, because in exchange for room and board, she was given chores around the house and garden. Sometime during those weeks, Mary came across Farmer Dolan's .22-caliber revolver. Maybe she hid it under her mattress for a few days while she thought about what to do. Maybe she made an immediate decision. Whichever, on June 13 she went out to the garden, picked some flowers, and tied her legs together with black ribbon. She then placed the flowers between her feet and shot herself in the right temple.

Luckily (or not, considering what was to come), Mary Delmar survived. The Dolans took her to Lewistown Hospital, where she was treated for an eye injury; possible brain damage was diagnosed. The nurses and interns at the hospital thought she was a mental case, but one Dr. Brown was not so sure.

"She answers questions very well," Dr. Brown wrote in his report, "until you come to the point where you begin to question her concerning her past life, when she immediately develops a headache and does not recollect." Dr. Brown believed that "she has some connection that she does not wish to divulge," and that she may be "communistic," as she had no use for the rich.

No doubt Mary Delmar has had a nervous breakdown. But she is in enough control of her emotions to hide what she wants to hide. It will develop that her real name is Rywka Brokowicz. And soon she will have a visitor—one Amy Mac-Master, a woman to whom she was previously unknown, and in whose custody she will be released from the hospital.

Juliet Poyntz now enters the story. It turns out that Amy MacMaster is acting on Poyntz's behalf. The FBI suspects that Delmar—or Brokowicz, as I will now call her—is a woman known to them as Lena. They believe that Lena is the Soviet recruiter of, and contact for, Juliet Poyntz.

Rywka Brokowicz will soon drop out of this story, but let's follow her as far as possible. At Poyntz's request, and for a payment of $25 a week to cover expenses, Amy MacMaster takes charge of Brokowicz. Eighteen years later, MacMaster will tell the FBI that she took Brokowicz home with her to Washington, D.C. But, unable to deal with the distraught woman, she placed her in a Philadelphia hospital. When Poyntz came to visit, Mac-Master witnessed Brokowicz becoming violently agitated.

Poyntz took over the situation. She obtained passports for MacMaster and Brokowicz and booked passage for them on the *Normandie,* sailing for France. She arranged for the two women to be accompanied on the ship by Dr. Julius Littinsky and his wife, Tilly. The foursome set sail on September 2, 1936. When they arrived in Paris, MacMaster remained with her companions for three days; then, leaving Brokowicz with the Littinskys, she returned to the States. Poyntz had told MacMaster not to worry; the Littinskys would turn Brokowicz over to "friends from Poland."

Who are the Littinskys? When questioned by the FBI in 1953, they will reluctantly acknowledge that Poyntz did ask them to befriend the two women, but they claim that they had only the most casual contact on the ship and, once in Paris, did not see the women at all. At the time he makes this statement, Dr. Littinsky is chief medical examiner for the International Workers Order and treasurer of the Morning Freiheit, both institutions closely associated with the Communist Party. He denies, however, that he was ever a Communist. He and his wife, Tilly, say they barely knew Poyntz, although Mrs. Littinsky thinks she saw Poyntz on the pier the day they sailed for France. The Littinskys also say that the purpose of their trip abroad in 1936 was to celebrate their twentieth wedding anniversary; after a brief stay in Paris, they had traveled by train through Germany and Poland and then on to the Soviet Union, where they visited relatives.

Goodbye to Rywka Brokowicz. We can hope that she was merely an unstable woman to whom Juliet Poyntz extended a disinterested helping hand; and that once in Poland, or wherever she landed, Rywka was reunited with the little boy whose photograph she carried from the train. Faint hope. This was 1936; by then Juliet Poyntz had been recruited as a Soviet agent, and she had shepherded Rwyka to the East just as the terror of Stalin's purges were about to peak.

Juliet Poyntz was an American girl born in Omaha in 1886. She was extremely well educated for any time, but particularly for her own. She earned an undergraduate degree from Barnard and a master's degree from Columbia University, and she won a fellowship for further study at the London School of Economics and Oxford. She was intelligent and high-minded. Early in her undergraduate days, she had become interested in social questions, particularly in matters of poverty and immigration, and in 1909 she joined the Socialist Party.

Photographs taken when she was a young woman show that Poyntz was an attractive woman, though somewhat spoiled for beauty by a heavy jaw. By all accounts she had compelling light brown eyes, a charming smile, and impressed everyone she met by the force of her character, her self-confidence, and her incisive intelligence. While she was studying in England, Poyntz met Friedrich Franz Ludwig Glaser, the heir to a German industrial fortune. Poyntz and Glaser came back to the United States together in 1913 and were soon married. The marriage lasted only a few years, but they never divorced and were still legally married in 1935, when Glaser died.

By the time Poyntz was forty, she was a personage in the world of radical politics. She had taught history at Columbia University, coauthored a book about the labor movement, been appointed director of education for the International Ladies' Garment Workers' Union, lectured for the Socialist Party, joined the Communist Party in 1921, and was a teacher at the Communist Workers' School. In 1924 the Party ran her as a candidate for Congress.

Everyone in the Party knew Poyntz. Whittaker Chambers, attending his very first Party meeting in 1925, left an indelible glimpse of Poyntz as she was in her late thirties: a heavyset, handsome, softly feminine woman who rose from her seat during the meeting to answer the remarks of the previous speaker. Calmly, and with impressive authority, she made the observation "The comrade is a liar."

For Party members, there was no such thing as an honest difference of opinion. A few months earlier, Poyntz had had this fact impressed on her. Finding herself on the losing side of one of the Party's internecine battles, she had been accused of "crimes of the highest order." At one point her views attained the status of an ism, as when the Party called for the liquidation of "Poyntzism." Her closest comrades, who had also backed the wrong side, were expelled. Poyntz was allowed to remain, but only after she had disavowed her previous views and sworn that from that moment on, she would follow the policies of the Comintern, no matter her own inclinations. In the years that followed, she was placed at the forefront of the Party; she ran for various public offices on the Party ticket; she frequently addressed cheering crowds and lectured to admiring students, none more attentive and admiring than the darkly pretty young woman who was my mother-to-be.

With all her many occupations, Poyntz often found time to travel abroad. Between 1921 and 1936, she applied for and received six passports: four in the name of Poyntz, two in the name of Glaser. In each passport application, she swore that her previous passport had been lost or, alternatively, that she had never been issued a passport. In her 1929 application, for instance, she wrote that the passport issued to her the previous year "was packed with numerous papers and books in a hurry and therefore carelessly in a rickety trunk that has been moved several times since last year . . . and evidently dropped out of the broken end of the trunk to my great regret since I have to pay $10 for a new one . . ."

Six passports are a lot of passports for one person. We would not be deviating from known facts if we were to infer that Poyntz's superfluous passports were turned over to Soviet-trained forgers and used as "boots" by comrades who preferred not to travel legally—specifically to the Soviet Union, or on Soviet business.

Poyntz was, herself, spending a significant amount of time in the Soviet Union. How do we know this? In August 1931, a flyer posted in Terre Haute, Indiana, advertised her as a lecturer who offered "the opportunity of a lifetime to hear about the wonders of WORKERS RUSSIA by the most brilliant woman speaker in the American labor movement WHO HAS JUST SPENT A YEAR IN SOVIET RUSSIA."

On April 8, 1934, using a passport issued in the name of Juliet Glaser, Poyntz sailed aboard the *Europa* on the first leg of another journey to Moscow. When she returned home early in the fall, friends noticed a change in her behavior. No longer was she the public face of the Party; nor did she attend Party meetings anymore.

She was not in hiding: friends and acquaintances ran into her from time to time and she was perfectly cordial. But she kept an uncharacteristically low profile, and those who knew how to read the signs believed that she had been recruited for "special work," which meant she was now an agent of Soviet intelligence.

In the mid-thirties, Poyntz lived in a brownstone apartment on the windswept corner of Seventy-fourth Street and Riverside Drive. She sometimes gave parties there, specifically to meet Columbia students; she also frequented the university's International House. She particularly wanted to become acquainted with Italian and German students, whom she attempted to recruit as agents to work for the Soviets when they returned home.

Elizabeth Bentley, who was a member of the Party and had spent some time as a student in Italy, was among those approached by Poyntz. Bentley was suspicious of Poyntz and refused her suggestion that she work in Italy with the anti-Fascist underground. But Poyntz had not been far off the mark in thinking the young woman was a likely recruit: Bentley would later work for the Soviet agent Jacob Golos, as a courier to a Washington spy network that included Alger Hiss; after Golos died, she ran the network herself. In 1945, when Bentley confessed her activities to the FBI, she told them among much else (including the name of a Julius who turned out to be Julius Rosenberg) of having been approached several times by Juliet Poyntz. But by that time Poyntz was eight years gone.

In October 1936—a little over a month after she stood on the pier, watching as Rwyka Brokowicz sailed to her fate on the *Normandie*—Poyntz, using her most recently issued Juliet Glaser passport, sailed once more, probably to the port of Riga, in Latvia, to make her way to Moscow. Think of it: Moscow in the winter of 1936–37. The first of the purge trials had taken place the previous August, ending with the death penalty for all defendants. The second wave of terror was about to burst, and this time it would include Stalin's agents in foreign countries, many of whom had received a summons "home."

Whittaker Chambers was called "home" to Moscow in 1937; he stalled and began to plan his defection. Ignatz Reiss, a high-ranking NKVD agent who had worked for Soviet intelligence in Spain, was called "home," broke with Stalin instead, and was assassinated in Switzerland. Walter Krivitsky, another high-ranking agent, defected after Reiss's murder and was found dead in mysterious circumstances in Washington a few years later. Theodore Stepanovich Mally, a Hungarian who had served the Soviet cause since World War I, was summoned "home." Ignatz Reiss's wife asked Mally why he was going to certain death. Out of guilt, he told her: guilt for the terrible things he had seen and done in Stalin's service. Jacob Golos, Elizabeth Bentley's superior, also stalled when he was recalled, and managed to die of natural causes.

Poyntz must have been filled with trepidation when she sailed that October. Miraculously, she returned to New York in February. She had escaped death. But, as she told an old friend, the anarchist and longtime anti-Stalinist Carlo Tresca, her faith had been shaken. While she had been in Moscow, her own loyalty had been questioned; somehow she had managed to allay suspicion but had been assigned to interrogate others. No doubt, like other interrogators, she learned how false confessions were obtained. To another old friend, Ludwig Lore, who had been expelled from the Party years earlier, she said that it no longer seemed possible for her to continue with underground work. She didn't know what to do.

Poyntz made no public statement of disaffection. She believed that she had a little time to figure things out—seven months, in fact. According to the return ticket found among her belongings, she had a third-class reservation aboard the *Britannic,* due to sail from New York on September 18, 1937. She was expected back "home."

On leaving New York in October, Poyntz had given up her apartment on West Seventy-fourth Street. She now lived in a studio apartment at the American Women's Association Club-house, on Fifty-seventh Street, near Tenth Avenue.

Toward the end of May 1937, Poyntz went to see her lawyer, Elias Lieberman. She told him that she was badly in need of money. Her husband, Friedrich Glaser, had died two years previously, and Poyntz, as his widow, was trying to collect from his estate. Lieberman told Poyntz that he thought he could get her an advance of about $1,000 from the estate. He would prob-ably have the money for her by early June.

During the last week of May and the first days of June, Poyntz was seen in New York by a number of people: Carlo Tresca, whom she had met by chance and to whom she had con-fided her disillusion; Ludwig Lore, whom she saw frequently; Sophia Theis, another old friend, who later told the FBI that she had lunched with Poyntz in late May. Poyntz had told her, "I have extricated myself from my former connections and I am now going to do some writing." When Poyntz and Theis parted after lunch, they made a date to meet two weeks later.

On June 4, Poyntz had an appointment with a Dr. Worces-ter that she failed to keep. Elias Lieberman expected to hear from her that week about the money she desperately needed. She did not call him, and he was unable to reach her by phone. Lieberman was accustomed to her habits of travel, which was why, he told police, he did not report her missing for six months.

It was December 1937 when Lieberman, pressured by other friends of Poyntz's, finally went to the police. A detective was sent to Poyntz's apartment. He found her clothes hanging in the closet, her lingerie folded in the drawers, her luggage empty, her passport in a desk drawer. A bowl of Jell-O had long since gone to liquid on the kitchen table. Her trunks, which she had stored at a warehouse, contained only books and notebooks that outlined material for a projected history of modern Europe.

In mid-December a report of Poyntz's disappearance appeared in the New York newspapers. A reporter asked the Communist Party for a comment; the Party's New York State membership secretary said there was no record that the woman had ever been a member of the Communist Party.

Not another word was ever heard of Juliet Poyntz. The switchboard operator where she lived reported that a man with a deep voice, who had often telephoned her, did so again on the morning she disappeared. Soon after that phone call, Poyntz left her apartment. A year later, a grand jury was convened to hear testimony on her disappearance. A number of people had theories to offer—especially that she had been lured by an old lover to a Russian ship then docked in the harbor. As it turned out, no solid leads developed, and the investigation reached a dead end. Not many months later, the Soviet spymaster Colonel Boris Bykov rhetorically asked his agent Whittaker Chambers, "Where is Juliet Stuart Poyntz?" Delighted with his mastery of the American idiom, Bykov answered himself gaily, "Gone. Gone with the wind."

Seven years later, Poyntz's sister went to court to have Juliet declared legally dead. Very few details of the above story were known to my family, but enough were suspected to cause consternation in our house.

Jury Duty

On the morning of September 10, 1976, Jerome B. Mandel was sitting at his desk in his small beige-painted office in downtown Brooklyn. He was doing some paperwork on one of his cases, and he was hoping that his phone would ring.

Jerome (Jerry) was a criminal defense lawyer, a lone practitioner, small-time. Jerry himself was quite small, if pigeon-plump. And if he hadn't been to an Ivy League law school, and he didn't get the big-money cases, he was nevertheless a member of the bar, and his job was—as defense lawyers like to put it when they appear on television—to put the prosecution's proof to the test. This is a good job. It's mandated by the Constitution.

On that morning of September 10, Jerry Mandel's phone did ring. The conversation went something like this:

"My boy's in trouble."

"What kind of trouble?"

"They're saying he killed somebody."

Jerry Mandel reached for his yellow legal pad: the boy's name was Mark Simon, age seventeen; the victim was Charlie Houston, age twenty; the place was Morningside Park, in Harlem; the name of the investigating homicide detective was Robert Abrahamsen. Mandel got a sense of this case, which was similar to other cases he had handled, and in the course of this first conversation, he mentioned his fee. Experience had taught him that in cases like this, you'd better get your money up front.

September 8, 1976 (two days before Mandel's phone rang), was a hot, sunny day, just cooling off a little in the late afternoon. Mark Simon, who was known as Spooky to his friends, was riding around his Harlem neighborhood on a ten-speed bike. At about five o'clock, he turned the corner of his home block, which was 114th Street, between Eighth and Manhattan avenues. It must be said that these were bad years for the city; the crime rate was soaring, the streets were full of uncollected garbage, the infrastructure was in a general state of decay. As usual, things were worse in black neighborhoods than they were in the rest of the city, and that particular stretch of Eighth Avenue was burned out and vandalized. But 114th Street was mostly habitable, lined with six-story tenements, only a few of which were abandoned.

At that hour, and in such fine weather, there was a lot of activity on 114th Street. Children were playing games outdoors, windows were wide open, and women leaned out to shout to their children or call to neighbors on the stoops below. At a row of garbage cans on the east end of the block, four or five boys were gathered, among them Charlie Houston and his younger brother, Ben. Mark Simon knew them. He stopped his bike.

"Can I have a ride, Spooky?" said twenty-year-old Charlie Houston.

Mark agreed and handed over the bike. Charlie mounted, rode off, and returned a minute or two later. It was clear to everyone why he had come back so soon: the bike's rear tire had gone flat. Who was responsible for this? Charlie and Spooky exchanged angry words. Manhood was impugned. There were demands for money. Pushing and shoving occurred. The situation was not resolved.

A couple of hours later and a couple of blocks to the west, in the raised cement play area of Morningside Park, an area that runs between 116th and 119th streets, a basketball tournament was in progress. A few minutes after seven o'clock, when the games were in the last minutes of play, gunshots were heard. The games stopped. Heads swiveled toward the sounds. Clamorous voices distilled into screams.

Later, it would be estimated that between 70 and 150 people—spectators and players—filled the basketball courts that day. But when witnesses were questioned, only a few would admit that they had noticed anything unusual. One witness reluctantly agreed to talk to the police. His name was Lynwood Hicks.

Hicks, who was acting as a coach for one of the teams, said that he had heard the shots, looked up, and saw a man running toward the 119th Street end of the courts. The running man took a zigzag course, bumping against the fence as he ran (a cyclone fence surrounded the park), trying to evade the gunshots. He was evidently headed toward a large hole cut in the fence near the north end of the park.

As for the shooter, his physical description varied, depending on the witness. But all witnesses agreed with Lynwood Hicks to this extent: that as the victim tried to escape through the hole in the fence, the shooter crouched, took a two-handed grip on his gun (a black gun? a silver gun? a .38-caliber? a .45?), aimed deliberately, and fired again.

By that time the victim had reached the hole in the fence. He disappeared from view, having jumped or fallen to the sidewalk several feet below. And then, said Lynwood Hicks, the shooter tucked his gun into his belt, turned south as the crowd parted for him, and walked swiftly out of the park. The incident was over. The light was failing. The players resumed the game.

About twenty minutes later, Officer Robert Paz arrived at the park. He found Charlie Houston's body under a lamppost, below the hole in the fence. Charlie's pockets contained $18 and change; no weapon, or anything else of significance, was found on or near the body.

At about that moment, Charlie Houston's younger brother, Ben, was once again on 114th Street. As Ben sat on the lid of one of those garbage cans, he saw Spooky walking toward him from the direction of Morningside Park. Mark Simon didn't stop, but he slowed, and as he approached Ben, he glanced at him and muttered:

"I shot Charlie, but not to kill him."

So that was Jerry Mandel's case. Not an untypical case in a year when there would be more than 1,600 murders in the city. What was this one about? About a perceived insult to manhood? About a flat tire that could have been fixed with two or three dollars? About nothing. Or everything, depending on local codes of behavior. I'm told there are blood feuds in the Balkans that get passed along from generation to generation, until no one alive can recall the original dishonor. Anton Chekhov once wrote to his brother, "People must not be humiliated, that is the main thing."

In this case, the bar for humiliation seemed to be set pretty low, and the deeds required to maintain respect—or primacy—on the streets of Harlem pretty extreme. Still, Harlem is not some mountain fastness; almost everywhere, murder is considered the great human transgression. And when a killer is brought to trial, it is the great human drama. Citizens are summoned to render justice (or, if you like, to write the end of the play). In any case, I was summoned.

Mark Simon sat at the defense table, cloaked in the presumption of innocence. He was barely eighteen, a very dark-skinned boy, about five-seven, well built, broad through the shoulders, his hair worn in a well-trimmed medium Afro. On that first day, as through most of the trial, he slumped or lolled in his chair, pretending ease. The only sign of fear could be read in his lips, which moved constantly as he chewed on the inside of his mouth.

Next to him sat his lawyer, my first sight of the aforementioned Jerome Mandel. (I must tell you that if I seem to know more than a juror would be able to glean at a trial, it is because I was dissatisfied, consumed with curiosity about the hints of background events that never made it into open court. In short, I developed doubts about the verdict. So when the trial was over, I asked Jerry Mandel and Robert Abrahamsen and the prosecutor, Lothar Genge, to tell me what had been left out of the evidence on which the jury based its decision.)

* * *

When Charlie Houston's brother, Ben, heard Mark Simon mutter his confession—"I shot Charlie, but not to kill him"—he went to the police. That same night, Ben, together with homicide detective Robert Abrahamsen, searched the neighborhood, looking for Mark Simon. They didn't find him that night or the day after. But on September 10, Jerry Mandel placed a call to Robert Abrahamsen.

"I hear you're looking for my client," Mandel said. "You've got the wrong guy." Mandel repeated what Mark Simon had told him: "My client says a guy named Donny Wilkens was the shooter."

As it happened, on the fateful night of September 8, Donny Wilkens, who was a tall, husky young man, had flagged down a gypsy cab for a ride across town. When the cab stopped for a red light on Lenox Avenue and 116th Street, two men approached the cab and shot Donny Wilkens fifteen times, killing him instantly.

Abrahamsen wasn't buying the Donny Wilkens story. Later, he said, "Donny Wilkens was a bad actor. He had a lot of enemies. His killing was supposed to be over an argument he'd had about a girl earlier that day. I didn't think he had anything to do with Charlie Houston's murder."

Abrahamsen wanted Mark Simon, and three days later Mandel surrendered his client. Abrahamsen asked Mark Simon if he wanted to make a statement.

"No, sir," said Mark Simon.

Abrahamsen arrested him for the murder of Charlie Houston. The next day Mark Simon was arraigned and was back on the street on $5,000 bail.

Abrahamsen started looking for witnesses among the people who had been at the basketball court. Most of them said they had seen nothing. Abrahamsen was skeptical, to say the least: "A

Harlem kid has to notice. He's got to notice to survive. He's got to look at the guy with the gun so he can make sure he's not going to get it next. He's got to see which way the guy with the gun is headed so he can get out of the way. They know everything on those streets."

Eventually Abrahamsen came up with one eyewitness, a teenager named Howard James who lived in the neighborhood. Howard James said that he had seen Mark Simon shoot Charlie Houston on the basketball court. He was positive about it.

The other witness, Lynwood Hicks, was twenty years old. He was a college student, he had no criminal record, he did not live in the neighborhood, and he did not know Charlie Houston or Mark Simon or Donny Wilkens. Hicks was reluctant to tell Abrahamsen anything. He was scared. Nevertheless, he described the shooter as short, slightly built, dark-complexioned, and between twenty and thirty years old. The shooter had worn his hair in a close-cropped Afro, and he'd been armed with a large black gun. He might have been wearing a green jacket, but Hicks was not positive. When Hicks was shown an array of photographs that included Mark Simon and Donny Wilkens, he was unable to make an identification. But the description he gave of the shooter more closely resembled Mark Simon than Donny Wilkens, who was taller, huskier, older, and wore distinguishing sideburns and a beard.

With the positive identification from Howard James and Ben Houston's statements, a prosecutor was assigned to the case. This was Lothar Genge, who presented the case to a grand jury. On October 1, the grand jury handed down an indictment charging Mark Simon with murder.

· · ·

Genge and Detective Abrahamsen were now working closely together. They both knew that with only one eyewitness identification, the case was weak. Abrahamsen continued trying to find other witnesses: "Ben Houston told me that a guy named Richard had been standing right next to him when Mark Simon said that he'd shot Charlie. Ben said that Richard had heard the confession. So I reach out for Richard. And Richard says he doesn't want to get involved. He doesn't own up to being there."

Instead of talking to Abrahamsen, Richard called Jerome Mandel.

"One day in January I get this call: 'Hey, man, this is Richard.' He's calling from a phone booth, and he tells me that Abrahamsen has been hassling him to be a witness, and that Ben is putting pressure on him too. So I say to him, 'Come on down to my office!' Because if the D.A. wants to talk to Richard, I sure want to hear what the guy's got to say."

Richard told Mandel that although he had not actually overheard Mark Simon's confession, Ben had repeated it to him just after it was made. Mandel was not happy, but things could be worse: "It wasn't admissible evidence; it's hearsay."

Mandel called Lothar Genge: "'I hear you're looking for Richard. He's in my office now.'

"Genge nearly dropped dead," Mandel said gleefully. "His new witness turns up at my office! I told Genge what Richard said, and Genge said, 'I don't care what he says. I'm going to have him picked up as a material witness.'"

Lothar Genge, as tall and pale and thin as Mandel was short, dark, and plump, had been with the D.A.'s office for eight years, and he had some experience with reluctant witnesses. "Richard insisted that he had not actually overheard the statement, but who knows? What he did say was that just after Mark Simon passed by the garbage can where Ben Houston was sitting, Ben came over to him and told him what Mark had said: 'I shot Charlie, but not to kill him.' Richard said that Ben was really shaken."

The rules of hearsay evidence are too complicated for a layperson to understand, but in this case Genge couldn't introduce Richard's statement, even though it was confirmation of Ben's testimony. Still, Richard's statement increased Genge's confidence in his case.

"I never thought Ben had made up that confessional statement of Mark Simon's," Genge said. "It was too subtle; it exonerated Mark Simon of the legal charge of murder, while it still implicated him in the shooting. Ben wasn't capable of that. And here was Richard, who in no way wanted to get involved, who admitted to hearing about the confession immediately afterward."

On the night of Charlie Houston's death, Abrahamsen had been given the name of another possible eyewitness: a nineteen-year-old named Evelyn. Evelyn had two children who lived with Evelyn's mother in the Bronx. Evelyn lived wherever she could. "She'd call her mother every couple of days to see how her kids were, but she never went home. She'd live here one day, then pick up and move," Abrahamsen said. After hearing her statement, he brought Evelyn to Genge's office.

"Evelyn was not what you'd call an ideal witness," Genge said. "She had a record. She'd also been known to call herself Sharon Tate. But about this incident, she was very clear, very definite."

Evelyn had been at the basketball court; she had seen the shooter. He came into the park by himself. She saw him take a shot at Charlie while Charlie was playing basketball, just as Howard James had described. She saw Charlie running the zigzag course that Lynwood Hicks had described. Then she saw the shooter crouch, take the two-handed grip, and fire twice more with a black gun. She saw him only in profile, but her description matched the description Hicks had given—a short, slight young man with broad shoulders, wearing a light green jacket, his hair in a short Afro. Evelyn thought he was younger than the twenty-to-thirty age range Hicks had given. She thought he was about seventeen.

Abrahamsen tested her on the age question. "How old do you think I am?" he asked.

"Thirty-five," Evelyn said, getting it right.

But when Evelyn was shown an array of twelve photographs that included pictures of Mark Simon and Donny Wilkens, she picked out Donny Wilkens without hesitation. She said that Wilkens had been in the park. She knew him. Wilkens had once raped her girlfriend. And because she knew Wilkens and was terrified of him, she kept her eye on him. Wilkens, who had been wearing a black leather jacket and a white baseball cap, had left the park a few minutes before the shooting. He was definitely not the shooter, she said. But she wasn't sure that Mark Simon was either; in the photograph she was shown, Mark's hairline was different from her memory of it.

All exculpatory evidence must be turned over to the defense, and since Evelyn was unable to identify Mark Simon, Genge gave her name to Mandel.

"Evelyn cut both ways," Mandel said. "She couldn't identify Mark, but she said Donny Wilkens wasn't the shooter. If the prosecution had brought her on as a rebuttal witness, I'd have screamed objections: 'How did she know Donny had raped her girlfriend? Was she there?' I was prepared to neutralize her testimony."

But Evelyn never testified at the trial. Soon after her name was given to Mandel, she stopped returning Abrahamsen's calls and couldn't be found.

The prosecution had one last bit of information. At about eight P.M. on the night of Charlie Houston's death, a boy named David was standing in front of the Golden Skillet restaurant on 114th Street and Eighth Avenue. He'd seen Mark Simon, Mark's friend Otis Rivers, and a third person get into a gypsy cab.

In the months before the trial, Jerome Mandel waited for his client's witnesses to appear. "My client assured me that he had witnesses who would testify that he wasn't the shooter." Mandel was still waiting at the end of December, when Genge starting pushing the case for trial.

"Genge starts screaming that we should raise my client's bail. He's saying his witnesses are being threatened. He says, 'We don't want these people down on the streets settling it among themselves. Let's have a quick trial.'

"Well," Mandel said, "I didn't want that. I wasn't ready for trial. Frankly, I didn't have the witnesses at that point."

At last Mark Simon produced three witnesses: Rafael, who said he'd been told by Donny Wilkens himself that Wilkens had shot Charlie; Otis Rivers, who said he'd seen Donny shoot Charlie; and Matty, who said that he too had seen Donny shoot Charlie. Mandel felt confident that, with two definite eyewitnesses who exonerated his client, he had a strong case. In February, Mandel's case became even stronger when Howard James, the only witness to positively identify Mark Simon as the shooter, recanted his testimony.

Genge was furious. "Now Howard is telling me that yes, he'd been in the park playing basketball, but that he never actually saw Mark Simon shoot the gun. He had come forward only because everybody in the neighborhood knew that Spooky did it."

Abrahamsen thought he knew very well what was going on. "This kid, Howard, is a fearful-type kid. Timid. I don't see him giving testimony that's a lie, but I can see him changing his mind when the guy he's testifying against is out on the streets. Bail has a dual function. It's supposed to protect society too. How are you going to conduct an investigation when witnesses are scared?"

What was Genge going to do? "Given the evidence we had even after Howard James recanted, I felt morally compelled to go to trial. Somebody had been killed. I felt I had legally sufficient evidence, but I wasn't sure a jury would be satisfied beyond a reasonable doubt."

The case was marked for trial in early February. Two days before, Mandel called Genge. To his surprise, Genge sounded "real blase about going to trial. I couldn't believe it! Was this the same Lothar who was gangbusters to start? I went up to his office, and he's, like, very depressed. He says to me, 'Look, frankly I haven't got much. Give me a good witness who says that Donny did it, and we won't go to trial.' "

Mandel decided that fourteen-year-old Matty, who said he had seen Donny Wilkens shoot Charlie, was his most credible witness. "I thought Genge would take Matty's statement and maybe throw the case out. But Matty messed around. I couldn't get him to go down to Genge's office."

While he waited for Matty to appear at his office, Genge read the notes of Mandel's interview with Matty. Matty had told Mandel that the shooting had taken place at the entrance to the basketball court, a statement that flatly contradicted both Lynwood Hicks and Evelyn, both of whom placed the shooter far into the court.

"Okay," Genge said to Mandel. "We're going to trial."

On Tuesday, March 1, the jury, my jury, began to hear evidence.

We would never hear Howard James identify Mark Simon as the shooter.

We would never hear Evelyn insist that Donny Wilkens was not the shooter.

We would never hear Richard confirm Ben Houston's statement about Mark Simon's confession; nor would we hear David testify that he had seen Mark Simon and Otis Rivers get into a cab together when both would claim to have been somewhere else. ("The last I heard of David," Genge told me, "he was in the intensive care unit of Harlem Hospital with stab wounds.")

Nor did Matty or Rafael—both of whom had told Mandel that Donny Wilkens was the shooter—testify for the defense. "Matty showed up for the trial," Mandel said later, "but he was spaced out. The kid was like a zombie, I couldn't put him on the stand." And Rafael? "He never showed up at all."

What was left of the case?

Ben Houston, Charlie's younger brother, was the first to take the witness stand. He gave his age as seventeen. He was a stocky boy; he spoke slowly. He said that at five P.M. on September 8, he was sitting on the lid of a garbage can on 114th Street when Charlie returned Spooky's bike with the rear tire gone flat.

"Spooky asked Charlie for three dollars to fix the flat. Charlie said he'd give Spooky two dollars. They kind of pushed the bike at each other. Then I said I'd pay to fix the tire. Spooky said to me, 'That's not the principle. God gave him a gift, and he didn't know how to use it. I'm gonna kill Charlie.'"

Shortly after the incident with the bike, Charlie went to Morningside Park to play basketball, while Ben rode the streets on his own bike for a while. Then he rode back to 114th Street to keep a date with a girl named Debbie Parker.

Debbie Parker was a pretty girl, only fourteen but she looked older, not the least bit nervous, in fact very self-possessed. She said that, yes, on September 8 she had walked over to 114th Street to meet Ben Houston. She was early for their date; while she waited for Ben, she saw Mark Simon talking to another boy. She knew Mark. She went over to him.

"Hi, how you feeling, Spooky? Haven't seen you for a long time."

Spooky paid no attention to her and kept talking to his friend.

"Spooky was saying that he'd almost just put Charlie to sleep, and if he had done it once, he'd do it again. He said he had a gun. He'd been going to throw it away, but now he wouldn't. He'd use it on Charlie."

The evening was gathering speed. Debbie left the block at

about seven-thirty. Fifteen minutes later, Ben Houston was once again hanging around the garbage cans when he saw Mark Simon walk quickly up the street, coming from the direction of the park, heading toward Eighth Avenue. Mark did not stop, but as he approached Ben, he slowed down and muttered a sentence just loud enough for Ben to hear:

"I shot Charlie, but not to kill him."

That evening, after he learned that Charlie was dead, Ben led Robert Abrahamsen, of the Fifth Homicide Zone, on a fruitless search of the neighborhood for Mark Simon.

Lynwood Hicks took the witness stand. Before beginning his testimony, he asked the judge if the door to the corridor could be closed; he didn't want to be seen. He was an impressive witness, twenty-one years old, a college student majoring in occupational therapy; he worked in a community methadone program, was an outsider to the neighborhood, and knew no one involved in the case.

"I was standing on the sidelines watching the team when I heard sounds, like firecrackers or shots. I looked toward the north end of the court and saw this guy running a zigzag course. I saw this other guy running after him. He took aim and fired again. I turned my head away. When I looked back, this guy, the shooter, was walking in my direction and tucking his gun into his belt. The gun was a large one, black, a thirty-eight, maybe a forty-five. I got out of his path."

Hicks described the shooter: about five-seven, broad shoulders, short Afro. When asked if he could identify the defendant as the shooter, Hicks looked directly at Mark Simon for the first time.

"I'm not sure."

. . .

After three days of prosecution witnesses, Mandel opened for the defense. He had found a new witness, one whose existence he was unaware of until the trial was already under way: Joshua Sullivan, eighteen, a high school student, well-spoken, with no arrest record. Joshua had gone to the basketball court on September 8. He said that he and a girl whose name he did not know entered the court through the hole in the north end of the fence. They had been watching the games for about five minutes when he heard the shots. He saw the shooter crouched about three yards away.

He had a silver gun. He was about five-ten and husky, with sideburns and chin whiskers.

"No," Joshua said to Mandel's question about whether he knew Donny Wilkens.

"Did you know the defendant?"

"Yes, but I only saw him a few times at the house of this girl I was dating. He was dating her sister."

At this point the jury exchanged perplexed glances: this was our first clue that Mark Simon's defense was going to be "some other dude did it." Although we had no way of knowing that Joshua Sullivan was a surprise witness, we could see that Genge was angry.

"Did Mr. Mandel take notes during your interview?" Genge asked the witness.

"Yes."

Genge turned to Mandel. "May I see those notes, Mr. Mandel?"

"Certainly, Mr. Genge."

Genge read through the yellow legal pad and faced the

witness again. "I see here in Mr. Mandel's notes that you described the shooter as having a mustache."

He handed the notes to Joshua Sullivan, pointing to the relevant lines.

"That must be a mistake," the witness said.

"Oh, by the way, Mr. Sullivan, you said that the shooter was about three yards away from you. How many feet is that?"

"I don't know."

The penultimate witness for the defense was Otis Rivers, who acknowledged that he was a good friend of Mark Simon's and was at the basketball court on the fatal day.

"I saw Donny Wilkens shoot Charlie Houston."

For a week the jury had been studying Mark Simon—furtively, because the connection between us was too charged to acknowledge by open staring. He looked very young. Except for his hair, which was now neatly styled in a medium Afro (grown out, one might conjecture, from the short Afro described by witnesses), he matched exactly the descriptions given of the shooter by the prosecution witnesses.

For a week he had seemed affectless, paying no attention to the evidence, whether helpful or damaging to his case. He lolled in his seat, occasionally whispered to Mandel, constantly chewed on the inside of his mouth.

And now he was taking the stand. For the occasion, he was more formally dressed than he had been, wearing a three-piece gray suit with white stripes, a dark shirt, and a light patterned tie. He was also wearing black-rimmed tinted goggles. The goggles and the outfit were a mistake; he looked older, more menacing. The jury could hear Mandel whisper to him to take off the glasses.

He was a heavily coached witness, which may also have been a mistake.

"Yes, sir . . . No, sir . . . That's correct, sir . . . Then we proceeded to the corner . . ."

In response to Mandel's leading questions, he told the jury about his life.

"I live at home with my mother, father, my brothers, and three puppies . . . No, I don't go to high school anymore. I used to go to Charles Evans Hughes High School, but my father got sick and I had to quit to work in his trucking business . . . Yes, sir, I'm studying at night for my high school diploma."

As for the events of September 8:

"Charlie asked me for a ride on my bike. Charlie was a bully. He was always picking on younger, smaller kids . . . Yes, sir, I was afraid of him.

"When Charlie brought my bike back with the flat, I asked him to fix it. He says, 'Nobody tells me what I got to do.'

"I say, 'I'm not telling you what you got to do. You asked me for a ride like a man, I give you a ride like a man, you should fix it like a man.' "

Mark Simon denied that Ben Houston was present during this exchange. As for Debbie Parker, there was no way she could have overheard any conversation he had that afternoon. And besides:

"I used to mess around with Debbie, and then I broke up with her. She's got an attitude about me. She's going with Ben now."

After the incident with Charlie and the bicycle, Mark asked his friend Otis Rivers to go to Morningside Park with him. He was upset; he wanted to play some basketball to take his mind off the argument with Charlie. As he and Otis walked toward the park, they were joined by two other friends, one of them Donny Wilkens. They continued toward the park, walking in pairs, Donny and Mark together. Mark told Donny about his argument with Charlie. Donny shook his head and mentioned that he too had been in a fight that day. He said, "I just don't know what's happening with these guys. I just been hit across the dome piece with a baseball bat."

When the four friends arrived at the park, they stood on the sidelines watching the games. Soon Charlie Houston approached them with a basketball under his arm.

"I see you brought your crew with you," Charlie said to Mark.

"It's not like that," Mark replied.

Donny intervened. He said to Charlie, "Don't you ever get tired of messing with people? Why don't you pick on somebody your own size?"

"Don't pay him any mind. He's not worth it," Mark said, pulling at Donny's arm.

"I'm getting tired of him," Donny said as Charlie walked away. "I'm going to take care of it."

Donny followed Charlie. Mark saw them facing each other, taking threatening postures; he heard their voices raised. He saw Charlie lift the basketball he was carrying, as if to throw it in Donny's face. Donny stepped back a pace, took a pearl-handled silver gun from his belt, and shot at Charlie. As Charlie started running away, Mark and Otis Rivers quickly left the park.

"How did you feel about what happened?" Mandel asked.

"I felt bad. I felt like it was my fault, sir."

Once out of the park, Mark said, he and Otis Rivers separated. Mark headed down toward 110th Street, where his current girlfriend lived. But when he got to her house, no one was at home. He waited for about a half hour and then, still upset, he took a cab to a movie theater on Third Avenue and Eighty-sixth Street. When he got out of the movie, he called home. His mother answered the phone and said, "The police have been here looking for you. Better not come home. Go to your sister's house in Brooklyn. We'll get you a lawyer."

Mandel had attempted a portrait of a responsible young man, one who lived in a stable family with brothers and sisters and puppies, one who left school to help in his incapacitated father's business, who eagerly studied at night for his high school diploma, who was fearful of the neighborhood bully. Now it was Genge's turn for cross-examination, and he pretty much destroyed Mandel's presentation. Genge offered Mark Simon as a heroin dealer who had been arrested and convicted for possession. Then Genge submitted two documents from Mark Simon's former high school: one from a teacher who reported that Mark Simon had slapped her across the face; the other from an assistant principal who said that Mark had threatened her. It was for these offenses that he had been suspended from school.

Genge handed Mark the conviction sheet and the two school reports.

"Those things never happened," Mark Simon said.

Mandel's closing argument tried to wrap up all the loose ends. Ben Houston, Mandel said, knew that Donny Wilkens had murdered Charlie. It was Ben himself who had killed Donny in revenge. And then, Mandel suggested, Ben had decided that while he was at it, he'd take revenge on Mark Simon too, so he made up the story of Mark's confession.

I was flabbergasted. Ben had killed Donny Wilkens? Not a jot of evidence had been presented in support of such an idea. And if Ben knew that Spooky hadn't killed Charlie, why would he want revenge? In any case, we knew that when Donny Wilkens was murdered in a gypsy cab, Ben had been with Detective Abrahamsen, looking for Spooky. I had no idea that a lawyer was allowed to spin arguments out of thin air, and so carelessly, too.

The jury argued for thirty hours (with time off to eat and sleep in a motel room somewhere in Queens). We wondered: if Donny Wilkens had indeed been hit in the head with a baseball bat earlier in the day, why hadn't he used his gun against the person who had actually attacked him?

Whom should we believe? Lynwood Hicks, who had described a shooter resembling Mark Simon, and who was a stranger to everyone involved; or Joshua Sullivan, who'd said the shooter looked like Donny Wilkens, and that he knew Mark Simon, but only a little?

And exactly why, out of an estimated hundred people on the basketball court, many of whom knew both Mark Simon and Donny Wilkens, did so few come forward to exonerate Simon? After all, if Donny Wilkens had been the shooter, he was dead; there was no downside to implicating him. But if Simon was guilty, fear and street loyalty would be inhibiting.

After the first day, the jury was divided—nine to three for guilt.

One juror, a man, thought Ben Houston's behavior was

unnatural. Why hadn't Ben grabbed Mark Simon when he made his confession?

A female juror refused to believe Debbie Parker, because Parker was only fourteen and had clearly had sexual relations with Simon. No girl of that age who had done such a thing was a reliable witness.

I thought this: if Mark Simon hadn't taken the stand, or if he had said, "I wasn't there, I don't know what happened," we could not have found him guilty. But he had said he was there, and the story he'd told was incredible. I couldn't forget the image of Charlie Houston running for his life, and of the shooter crouching, taking deliberate aim, and shooting again. That was murder. But in the end, the jury could not agree on the murder charge. We compromised. We found Mark Simon guilty, not of murder but of manslaughter, based on the last phrase of his confession to Ben Houston: "I shot Charlie, but not to kill him."

When the jury came back into the courtroom for the last time, Mandel was staring at us. Genge stared at his tabletop. Mark Simon stared into space. At the "not guilty" verdict to the charge of murder, Genge slammed his fist into the desk. At the manslaughter verdict, he looked up, relieved. Mandel was distressed. "The least I expected with no eyewitness identification was a hung jury," Mandel said. "I shouldn't have lost this case."

Your fault, I almost said.

Mark Simon spent the next month on Rikers Island. During that month I went up to his neighborhood to look at the scene of the crime. I saw the basketball court, I saw the hole in the fence, I saw a graffito sprayed on a building wall along 114th Street. It read: JAIL SPOOKY.

On April 14, Mark Simon was back in the courtroom for sentencing. So were some of his friends and family. So were Mandel and Genge. So was I.

Mandel made a plea for a sentence of five years' probation on the grounds that Mark Simon was a youthful offender. The judge denied it. Mark Simon made his own plea for probation. He said that he wanted to help raise the baby his girlfriend was soon going to give birth to. The judge denied it.

Mark Simon was sentenced to nine years. At that time a nine-year sentence translated into a third of the time to be served in prison, with two thirds off for good behavior. So if he didn't get into trouble in jail, Mark Simon would probably be back on the street by the age of twenty-one.

I don't know anything about what happened to him after the day he told us about the baby who was going to grow up without a father.

Do you wonder if he took care of that baby when he got out of prison?

Do you wonder if he ever killed anyone else?

I sometimes wonder. I also wonder if, now that Mark Simon is forty-five, he's not a pillar of some community somewhere. That could happen. Or he could be dead.

All I know is that for a couple of weeks, his world and his young life opened to me. It was as if I had picked up a novel, a real page-turner, and while I read, the dishes piled up in the sink, the floor went unswept, the phone rang unanswered. I could think of nothing else until I'd finished the story. And when I reached the last page, I closed the book and put it on the shelf.

In the Vicinity of Art

The sign says Jersey Street, but that's too dignified a title for this leftover remnant of downtown real estate. Jersey Street is no more than an alley now, about as wide as the average living room, running two east-west blocks from Crosby Street to Mulberry. Sometimes you see a truck squeezing through, but no one lives on Jersey Street anymore.

I must have passed by Jersey a dozen times without noticing it. Then, one morning, as I was walking down Lafayette Street to have coffee on Prince Street, a shaft of early sun struck a brilliant diagonal down the alley. I glanced toward the sunlight. At that very moment a small white wirehaired dog trotted around the corner from Mulberry. The dog snuffled his way along the cobblestones, through sun and into shadow, headed for a puddle that had formed in a pothole; his short, squat owner waddled after him and stepped into the shaft of sun. At that moment—the decisive moment, as Cartier-Bresson named it—I raised my camera and took a picture. And what a beauty it turned out to be, with every tone that black-and-white film can render: the man outlined in sun; the dog halfway across the line from sun to shadow; the steel shutters of the buildings that usually darkened Jersey angled every which way, picking up glints of sun; and, in the background, still in soft shadow, the pretty chapel of Old St. Patrick's. If you ask me, this photograph is in the vicinity of art.

Of course, if you get onto the subject of art, everybody's a critic, and who am I not to have my own ideas? I like to look through those shoe boxes on flea market tables, the ones that overflow with the photographic detritus of lost lives. So often I'm struck by the beauty and the perfect framing of a snapshot. Is it art if it's an accident? Sometimes I see an image that is the definition of kitsch; as, for example, the postcard I bought of someone's beloved shepherd mutt. It was surely the dog's owner who had the snapshot hand-tinted and printed up as a postcard, and who, in 1912, stamped it, mailed it from Carson City, Nevada, and wrote the still-legible penciled message: "Please take good care of our dog." Imagine the narrative possibilities! A family flees town in the dead of night, leaving everything behind. To return? Never to return? What are their circumstances? What happens to them . . . to the dog? The postcard isn't art, but a writer who is touched by it might make art of it.

Or not.

I've been a critic, professionally. I've written reviews in my time, though never about fiction, certainly not about theater. I have my opinions about fiction and plays, but since I can't write either one, I don't feel competent to write about them. I write about nonfiction, on subjects I happen to know something about. I haven't always been kind to the writer. Sometimes a book just makes you mad.

But let's say that an old friend of mine, a dear friend, a playwright all his life, gets his play produced on Broadway. The play is highly acclaimed and my friend delights in his success. Since he is no longer as young as he once was, the moment is all the sweeter. He is sought out by interviewers who want to know about his play, and about his life. And often, when he gives these interviews, his wife, who is my best friend, is at his side. One day I come upon this passage in an interview he has given:

"Has the great success of your play had any effect on your life?" the interviewer asks my friend Nick.

"No, not really," Nick answers.

The interviewer has made no indication of it, but I'm pretty sure that at this point Nick will have paused and exchanged glances with Nora.

"But," Nick continues, "you learn that some of your friends rejoice at your good fortune, and others don't, which comes as a surprise and is painful."

As far as I know, there were no others who caused surprise and pain. There was only me. Mea culpa.

Listen, over the years I've lost lots of friends, to say nothing of other significant others. These things happen—people drift apart, irritations mount, an unforgivable betrayal occurs, whatever—there are dozens of reasons. But I never thought I'd lose Nick and Nora, and I couldn't have dreamed of the reason: I didn't like his play.

You didn't like his play? So *what*?

So what, indeed.

...

You know, I often wonder whether exceptionally attractive couples have a better time in bed than those of us of the more average persuasion. I suspect they do, don't you? Because in the Darwinian sense, they've hit the jackpot.

Nick and Nora were dazzling, anyone could see that. They were Olympian: tall, slender, beautiful, intelligent, witty. They were fifteen years into marriage when I met them, and crazy about each other, a dyad, not a sliver of separation between them. If they were poor, it was by choice. For art's sake, they had chosen poverty—if that was the way things went. All was not lost; art might yet provide.

Some of Nick's plays had been respectfully read, and some had been produced in off- and off-off-Broadway theaters. In the meantime they lived as cheaply as possible, earning money here and there at jobs that left Nick as much time to write as possible. Nick's life as a writer was the center of their lives, as much the center of Nora's life as it was of his. Not that there was anything recessive about Nora. *Au contraire.*

When we met—this would be in the mid-seventies—my circumstances were a little different. I wasn't married, not anymore. They had children, I had none. I was making a bare living writing freelance articles for women's magazines. My career ambitions were modest; I didn't think about being an artist. But we became friends, and along with lack of money, we had a number of other things in common: we agreed on politics, which included being against the Vietnam War and for civil rights, we held utopian hopes for a society organized on principles of justice, we had a tropism toward old-fashioned bohemianism. Also, we laughed at the same things.

But one thing was no laughing matter. Nick's genius.

One day early in our friendship, Nora said to me, "Nick is a genius."

She wasn't using the word lightly, as you might say to someone, "Oh, you found my glasses! You're a genius!" Or as you might use the word to mean that someone was really smart. No. Nora believed Nick was a genius; she didn't say that to everyone, she was making me a confidence. By implication, she was also telling me that not only had she chosen a genius, a genius had chosen her, which didn't make her chopped liver.

What did I think of it? I thought: Well, what do I know about genius? Einstein was a genius, but with my knowledge of physics, I had to take that on faith. Beethoven, Mozart, acknowledged geniuses, but I had a tin ear. Chekhov, Shakespeare: I know they were geniuses because I know how to read. Tom Stoppard: okay, yes. I had a good eye for painting (if it wasn't too abstract) and for photography, so I included Michelangelo and Cartier-Bresson and Saul Steinberg in my pantheon.

Nora gave me some of Nick's scripts to read. She gave me the script of his major unproduced play. I went with them to Alphabet City, where, on bare, unswept stages, actors sat around and read Nick's words. Was his genius apparent to me? Well, if enjoyment is a measure of greatness, I'd have to say that those experiences didn't give me much pleasure. But I felt handicapped: reading Nick's scripts, seeing them performed, made me nervous. Too much was at stake; our very friendship seemed to be at stake. And what I thought at the time was that I was too ignorant to understand the work. I assumed that what Nick was doing was beyond me—maybe it was avant-garde, maybe there was some aesthetic or literary principle that I just didn't get. Nick did what he did. So what if I didn't see the light? They were my friends.

It wasn't only Nora who thought Nick was a genius. This was something they agreed on, a foundation stone on which their marriage was built, and many of their friendships too. And even if the word "genius" took me aback, I had no doubts about Nick's intelligence, about his erudition. He was full of arcane knowledge, he read everything, he had large, complicated political and social theories, he could dredge up obscure, seemingly singular historical events and spin a cosmology that remade your understanding of the world. At least for the moment.

Nor was Nora a slouch. You should have heard them at dinner parties. They were a team, they flew on the wings of logic, and they never ever backed off an argument, especially not Nora, who could make mincemeat of anyone who disagreed. Argument was their delight, their sport. Sometimes a spectator sport.

Once in a great while, though, Nick would base an argument on a proposition that, by some fluke, I knew was flawed. Did I offer correction? Nope. I decided that I had probably misunderstood. Or, more accurately, I was afraid that my intellectual resources would drown in his deep water. And as for Nick's work, of course I praised it.

"Great," I said. "Great!"

Because isn't that what you say to a friend? And anyway I didn't have the nerve to say otherwise. Once, very tentatively, I asked Nora a question about one of Nick's plays—about a character who seemed less than plausible, or a plot line that confused me. Well, believe me, when I heard Nora's sigh of impatience, of contempt, really, I grew properly frightened. "I would grow properly frightened" is what Alfred Kazin said about his encounters with the mad Delmore Schwartz, not that I mean to imply Nora was mad. But fierce. Oh yes.

So you can see, can't you, that over the years these things accumulate? You dislike yourself for feeling intimidated: you become resentful of your friends, you blame your timidity on them when it's nobody's fault but your own. You draw back, you keep your reservations to yourself, you operate below the level of good faith. Mea culpa, as I said.

But don't forget that all this was sub-rosa. When these thoughts came to the surface, I pushed them away. I castigated myself for disloyalty. And for many years, we were having so much fun. Picnics, parties, a shared circle of friends. I had been floating in the world, unattached, and we became a threesome. They were the best of friends to me, loyal and loving friends. I published a book: they were happy for me. I had miserable love affairs: who else would I cry to? I had surgery: I counted on Nora. Our parents grew old and died: we went through that together. We went through life together.

And then Nick's luck began to change. One of his plays was produced off-Broadway and got good reviews. We four—by this time I had married—went to opening night together. We stood and cheered. We called, "Author, Author" as Nick took his bows. In fact, I had problems with the play—with Nick's style, which seemed self-conscious to me, with his language, which I thought self-insistent. I thought the situations and characters were contrived. It didn't matter. I was happy for them. Really. No reservations.

Nick was launched. He had a promise of a Broadway production for his new play. A year later it was finished. "It's genius!" Nora said to me. She was beside herself with happiness. She kept me au courant—and I mean several times daily—of each step in the production process: the stars who were eager for parts, the renowned director who had signed on, the producers who were investing big money. Everyone agreed: the play was genius . . . brilliant . . . thrilling . . .

I admit that I was getting a little nervous now. What if I didn't like it—and didn't I have reason to worry about that? The level of praise required for a major piece of work might be beyond my abilities. Also, I wanted to say, "Nora. Back off." I thought a little reticence on her part might be in order. I thought it might be a good idea for her to let the play speak for itself.

But reticence was not Nora's style, nor was "back off" mine. She was so certain, so convinced of Nick's genius; no one with an ounce of intelligence, an ounce of sensibility, could fail to see it for herself. Certainly not her best friend. Soon Nora had a treat for me. She put the script in my hands. She could barely wait for my expressions of joy.

Well, for the first ten pages or so, I felt huge relief. I thought, "Okay, this is good, this is working, I'm going to like this." But I read on and my heart sank.

There isn't much difference between reading a play and reading a novel. Reading is reading; when you're reading something good there comes a moment when the physical experience of looking at print dissolves and the work takes you over; you're deep into a journey. But reading a friend's work can never quite offer that experience. No matter how good the work is, disbelief can't be entirely suspended. You know the voice too well, you know where characters and events come from. As in this case. I knew where everything came from. These were not fictional characters to me. I knew them. I knew them as well as I knew my best friends. And I saw that the hero of my friend's play was a man who is a genius and something of a guru; also a moral giant who is generally irresistibly attractive to women, in particular to the beautiful heroine, who pursues him, understands and shares his qualities, and happens to be the only woman worthy of him.

What *was* my problem? Was this self-delight news to me? No. Nevertheless, I was shaken. When, in daily life, I find myself unsettled, I usually go shopping, but there is no distraction from art. They say that art can change you, and so it did. It was as if an optometrist had shifted lenses; in that split second I saw things differently. Of course, there were other elements to the play: the setting was imagined, the plot contained various interestingly imagined events. Still, my feelings had changed. I couldn't help it.

I was in despair, really.

"Great," I said. "It's just great!"

But I couldn't muster conviction. The play made me mad.

In view of subsequent events, you may legitimately ask me: "What do *you* know about art?" Because then the reviews came, prizes came, production companies were formed to take the play on the road, movie offers poured in. Yes, it *was* a great play! Everyone said so. And if I happened to miss a review, Nora sent it to me. My e-mail filled up with Nick's glorious reviews.

"Isn't this review wonderful?" Nora would e-mail. And I'd read the review and e-mail back, "Oh, yes. Wonderful." But I wasn't persuaded; I thought what I thought, and Nora wasn't fooled.

But this is what I kept asking myself: why should it matter?

Weren't Nick and Nora the same people, the same loyal and loving friends they'd always been? If, these days, in their happiness, there was some extra preening going on, a bit more holding forth at dinner tables, Nick's genius not such a tightly held secret anymore, so what? Wasn't euphoria perfectly natural?

But it did matter to me. And I asked myself what Nora later accused me of: was I jealous?

Because the time came when Nora said, "We know you've been resentful of Nick's success. You haven't been able to hide it . . . From the very moment of the first reviews you've made your feelings clear . . ." She held the moral high ground. Of course. What other ground does a wronged friend occupy?

I drank two martinis then. Gulp. Gulp.

Naturally that's what she would think. *They* would think. In their place I would have thought the same. You cast around for a reason why your best friend is not rejoicing in your happiness. What could it be? Jealousy. After all, wasn't I a writer too? Wasn't my husband a writer? Nothing like the acclaim that had come to Nick had been our portion.

But really I didn't think so, and how could I say what it was? It was fatigue. The long years of my own bad faith had exhausted me.

"You have a devil in you," Nora said.

I said, "I've ruined our friendship, haven't I?"

"Not if I can help it," said my generous real-life friend.

But I had. I felt sick.

Remember that photograph I took on Jersey Street? The dog, the man, sun and shadow. I was so pleased with it that I decided to do a series of Jersey Street pictures. Every day, or at least several times a week, in various weathers and different hours, I planned to stand on Jersey Street with my camera, just to see what passed by. I never did that.

Too bad. Because a while ago I found myself on the corner of Jersey Street again. For old times' sake, I stopped to look east toward Mulberry. It was a raw day in early spring. Fine rain fell from a polished pewter sky. At that very moment a nun in full regalia appeared on Mulberry Street. Three nuns followed behind her. Each nun carried a black umbrella. In the bright gray shadowless drizzle, they paraded in line past the pretty chapel of Old St. Patrick's. Think of it: four nuns in black-and-white habit; four black umbrellas held aloft; four umbrellas, four nuns, all tilted at identical angles into the wind. I didn't have my camera. In a moment they were gone. I felt sick. I had lost them.

Foucault's Last Lover

In the dead of winter, in the dark before dawn, my phone rang.

A slurred voice spoke: "*You . . . love . . . made you literary executor . . . left everything . . . you . . . my will . . . look in typewriter . . .*"

Clonk.

Were I to write a screenplay for this scene, you'd see a woman lying in bed in a dark room, her form beguilingly outlined by the faint street light that penetrates her window. You'd hear rain beating on the window, and then the jarring sound of a ringing telephone: brrrr . . . brrrr . . . brrrr . . . At the third ring, the woman rouses herself; groggy with sleep, she switches on a bedside light and reaches for the phone.

The scene shifts. A man in a brightly lit room is sitting on the edge of a bed. He speaks into a telephone. The camera moves in for a close-up, closer, closer, until the hand grasping the phone fills the screen. You watch as his hand loosens its grasp; in slow motion, an empty pill bottle drops to the floor, and the phone falls from his now-lifeless fingers.

Clonk.

A woman's voice crackles from the receiver on the floor: "Goddammit, Keppel!"

"Keppel," my friend Kitty said. "You should meet Keppel."

Keppel had been at Swarthmore with Kitty's husband.

I said, "Really? Isn't he married? I heard he was gay. You think he'd be interested in me?"

"He's separated," said Kitty. "He's not gay. Of course he'd be interested in you."

I told her the old joke: "Just because he's married and has two children doesn't mean he's gay."

Kitty laughed politely. "Anyway," she said, "you're beautiful, you're smart, and you're both writers. You could just meet him."

Kitty loved her friends exceedingly: none of us was less than beautiful, none of us had ever held a half-empty glass, none of us had a problem that wasn't a blessing in disguise. Kitty was an optimist; if you were a pessimist, as I happened to be, Kitty's worldview could drive you up the wall.

But it was true that when she mentioned Keppel, I perked up. I'd liked his book, which had to do with class. Social Class. I hadn't actually read his book, but I'd read about it, so I knew it was the kind of book that a person like me—a person who aspired to seriousness—should like.

Kitty gave an elegant dinner party, and late in the evening, long after I'd lost hope of him, Keppel strolled in. He was coatless (it was winter), with a cashmere scarf draped casually over his tweed jacket. I must say that I was somewhat taken aback. I had imagined a tall, thin, dark-eyed aesthete. Keppel was not short, but his body was soft and fleshy. He had the pale, waxy skin that is (unfairly, no doubt) associated with not washing very often. He had a few strands of brown hair. Large tortoise-shell glasses magnified his eyes. Soon I heard him laugh, the overloud laugh that comes a moment too late, from a person who doesn't really have a sense of humor; and I heard his voice, which was pitched high, in the rhythm of complaint.

I decided to cut him a break. You know the saying "Handsome is as handsome does"? Ridiculous. Everyone knows that handsome gets away with murder. In fact, that very evening at Kitty's dinner party, there was a very handsome man, married, who was making friendly overtures to me. I knew that would end in tears. I was a grown woman and I was ready to take other factors into consideration. In academic circles, Keppel was a celebrated man, a serious intellectual. That was attractive. I gave him a few minutes to notice me. He didn't. I called myself to his attention.

"I loved your book," I lied. "I'm so interested in class—Class."

There's a lame come-on for you.

"How nice," he said. "Are you?" His eyes scanned the room.

"Yes," Kitty said. "You know Dorothy's written a book about Class too." She told him the title.

Keppel looked at me with some interest. "Oh, is that your book! I loved it." In time I would learn that he had never even heard of my book, which, in any case, had not put me in his distinguished class (lowercase). But, as I had been identified as a published person, I was worth another glance.

Thus we two (let's call us flatterers, not liars; not yet) shared a taxi downtown to our respective homes.

"We should have lunch," Keppel said.

"Great!" I said. "Here's my number."

I waited three weeks before I called him. It's not that I never call men, but I prefer vice versa. I have learned that when a man says he'll call you and your telephone is silent, that's the message. But as I said, I'd made a decision: a man like Keppel was just the sort of man I needed. On paper, he was perfect.

I dialed Keppel's number, hoping to get his answering machine. He was home. There was no hint of recognition in his voice, even after I had identified myself by my first name and my last name. I still had to mention where we had met.

"Oh," he said. "I was just about to call you."

Such good manners. We arranged to have dinner. Everyone called him Keppel. His mother had named him, or so he often said, after Karl Marx. With or without this provenance, Karl was a perfectly good name, but for some reason, people had settled on Keppel. There was something comical about the name. In Yiddish, *keppel* means "head." "What a *keppele* on that child!" grandmothers boast about their grandchildren. But can you imagine saying, "I love you, Keppel"?

I don't think I ever said it. Not even in our most intimate moments (of which, yes, there were some). If I did say it, I refuse to remember, even though, for about a year, we were sort of a couple, Keppel and I. These many years later, I look back at that time and see that I was in a constant state of expostulation.

"But *why* did you tell me that you were going to Chicago and then tell Michael that you were in Philadelphia? Were you even out of town at all?"

"When that woman said she'd been to Choate, why did you say *you'd* gone to Choate when you told me you'd gone to public school?"

"I never lie," Keppel would say serenely each time he was caught in a lie. He lied all the time. He'd lie for self-aggrandizing reasons, or for some other advantage, social or professional, and he'd lie for absolutely no reason at all. Then he'd say something that I was sure was a lie, and it would turn out to be true. It was enough to send you screaming through the wards.

"Oh, but sweetheart, it's harmless," Kitty would say when I complained. "He doesn't hurt anybody, does he?"

But he did. Keppel loved to gossip. To gossip about the great and the near-great was to show his intimacy with them, to let you know that he was inside, knew their secrets. Often his gossip was a lie, sometimes innocuous, sometimes malicious, as when he told a story about a colleague whose new, widely reviewed book was, according to Keppel, plagiarized from someone else's work. What Keppel said got around, and the author of the book publicly and convincingly and angrily refuted the rumor.

"John Smith is furious at you! He heard that you're the one who said his work was plagiarized from Tom Jones. Why in God's name did you say that when you knew it wasn't true?"

"I never said that," Keppel said serenely.

"I heard you!" I expostulated.

Keppel's teaching schedule was very light, as befits a celebrated academic—maybe one seminar a week given to six elite postdoctoral students. The rest of the time he wrote monographs for scholarly journals and gave lectures that he delivered in great halls in various cities. He also arranged for important European intellectuals to come to New York, where he entertained them lavishly on his university funds. In return, they were expected to lecture and to participate in panel discussions organized by Keppel: discussions on culture and architecture, culture and politics, culture and sexual deviance, culture and class, culture and language. The culture part was American culture, which always came in for a drubbing from the Europeans. Keppel identified with Europeans. Sometimes he lost his English and had to search for it in French: "*Comment dit-on . . . ?*"

I went to some of these lectures. You're already aware that I am not an esteemed intellectual, a celebrated theorist, or even a lowly adjunct instructor. So what did I know? But I was quite struck to find that Keppel's personal anecdotes and ruminations were material for rigorous intellectual discourse.

"You know," Keppel said to a packed audience one evening, "I was walking up Broadway the other day when it struck me that there is a distinct relation between street signs as signifiers, and sexual self-esteem."

If those were not his exact words, I promise you they're not far off.

Keppel told me he was going to Paris to have discourse with his idol, Michel Foucault. I may have misunderstood him, because when Keppel returned, he began to casually mention around town that he had been Foucault's lover. Did he say "discourse" or "intercourse"? Who knew? The man would say anything. And that brings us to another matter.

It was true, as Kitty had said, that Keppel was separated from his wife when she introduced us. But was what I had heard true—that he was gay? The answer is that sometimes he was gay and sometimes he wasn't; it depended on the occasion. "We gay men and women," he once said to an audience composed of gay men and women.

"Keppel," I said, "do you like boys better than girls?"

He was indignant. "*Comment dit-on? . . . Non,* of course not." Which meant, I guess, that he liked girls better. "But," he said, and his eyes went soft and dreamy, "sometimes when you travel, you meet a beautiful boy, and you have a night out of time."

Very poetic.

A few months later, the world learned that Foucault was very ill. Soon Foucault died. This was the time when gay men were dying of a mysterious illness. It had no name, and it didn't occur to me that Keppel might have this illness, although he certainly complained enough about ill health. But a few months later, I decided I'd had enough of Keppel. The lying, the amorphousness of his nature, and my own fear of developing high blood pressure, or even a stroke, from constant expostulation. I was tired of trying to pin Keppel down. To say nothing of the sex business, of which I will say nothing. You must be wondering why I hung around so long.

The long and the short of it is, I had been in it for what I could get. Not for the jewels with which Keppel might cover me; no, I wanted him to lead me into the world of acknowledged intellectuals, to meet the great and the near-great, to see if I could hold my own among them. I had gotten about as much as I could get out of Keppel. I said goodbye. He took it very well. Actually, he hardly seemed to notice.

And then, a few weeks later, came the dead-of-night telephone call. After I'd yelled, "Goddammit, Keppel," I hung up the phone. I went to the window. Sleet was hitting the window-pane. It was three o'clock in the morning. There were no taxis on the Bowery. I called my friend Michael, who lived a few blocks away. He sounded very grumpy.

"Michael, Michael, I'm so sorry, but you've got to get your car and pick me up." I told him what had happened.

Michael knew Keppel. "Oh, please. He's putting you on," he said. But he knew we had to go. On the way over in the car, I was thinking, Gosh, suppose it's true. Suppose Keppel has killed himself and left me everything. It was not a displeasing thought.

"Should we call the police?" I asked Michael. "Should we call 911?"

"Just wait until we get over there," Michael said. "I think you'll find we won't have to call anyone."

We rang Keppel's bell. We heard sounds from inside. Michael rolled his eyes. Someone fumbled with the lock. Keppel opened the door. He looked bleary-eyed, drunk. We went inside. I glanced at the typewriter. Nothing.

"Keppel," I said, "are you all right?"

"I'm fine," he said. "I was at a party. I just fell asleep."

"Why did you call me?" I said.

"Yeah, why did you call her?" Michael said.

"I didn't call you," Keppel said serenely.

I should mention that by this time the world had learned the name of the disease that killed Foucault.

"Keppel," I said very gently, "I came because I was worried about you. You know, because of you and Foucault. Did you call me because you're afraid you have AIDS?" Just for the hell of it, I added, "Tell me the truth, Keppel."

Keppel's eyes widened. It never occurred to him that his

stories might have an afterlife. He'd almost forgotten the Foucault story, but now it was coming back to him. He was thinking about it, seeing how the story could play out, how his connection with Foucault might be engraved in history. Oh, he liked this idea!

"Yes," he said. "I went to the doctor today. He did some tests. I'll know the results in a few weeks."

Keppel smiled what he meant to be a brave smile. He was as serene as ever.

Stay

Our dog Harry briefly enjoyed a show-business career. Well, we enjoyed it. If Harry had a notion of celebrity, it had to do with food.

Harry's role, which was in a music video, was arranged by Phyllis, who was his trainer and walker, and who was also walker to a few dogs of the stars (Mary Tyler Moore's, Andie MacDowell's, Paul Simon's). Phyllis recommended Harry to play the part of Paul Simon's dog in a new song that mentioned a dog. We were thrilled but puzzled. First of all, why didn't Paul Simon use his own dog? If his dog wouldn't do, why not find one who more closely resembled the lyrics of his song, which called for a little dog? Harry was clearly medium-sized and weighed a muscular fifty-five pounds. More to the point, Harry was not reliable in the obedience department, as Phyllis had good reason to know.

The video actually got made. We saw a tape of it. And

since it is more than unlikely that you will ever see it, I'll describe it.

Simon's song is rather high-toned: it's about the French artist René Magritte and his wife, Georgette, who sought refuge in New York during World War II. In the video, we see the Magrittes, played by Paul Simon and his then-wife, Carrie Fisher, strolling arm in arm through Central Park, wearing clothes to evoke the forties: a bowler hat for Paul, a knee-length, chunky fur coat thrown over Carrie's shoulders. Their dog is at their heels and, as they stroll, we hear the song, which includes the phrase *"Mr. and Mrs. Magritte and their little dog after the war . . ."*

Paul and Carrie are more or less dressed for the part, but the hulking, shaggy black-and-white terrier mutt behind them must have escaped from another song. It is ludicrously obvious that the only reason Harry has agreed to follow these people is that in Paul Simon's free hand, which dangles by his side, there is a large biscuit. You can see the biscuit, which is just out of Harry's reach, and you can see that Harry is almost on tiptoe, straining his neck to the utmost, trying to get at it. Verisimilitude is shattered: this dog does not belong to that couple. In any case, the song never made the charts, and the video was the beginning and end of Harry's career, although we still speak of it, as we still speak of Harry.

From our courtship days, Ben spoke to me of dogs. Airedales were frequently mentioned.

"An Airedale, for instance. So companionable. He'd lie at your feet, his head on his paws, his eyes adoring you . . ."

I'd had a few dogs in my time, so I knew that passive adoration was only part of the picture. But I made the amateur debater's classic mistake by accepting my opponent's terms of argument.

"Airedales," I said, "cost hundreds of dollars. That's immoral when the shelters are filled with abandoned dogs."

"True!" Ben said happily. "So you agree, definitely a terrier."

Here's a riddle: when is an Airedale a red herring?

When we weren't talking about dogs, we talked about getting married. There was a small problem.

"Let's be sensible about this," Ben said. "We'll consult with Dr. Bruin."

Dr. Bruin was Ben's neurologist. The problem was that Ben had multiple sclerosis. His symptoms were still mild. Mildish. Trouble walking. Some days he could walk with two canes, some days he had to use a scooter. He could drive a car with hand controls, he could cook dinner, he could do a number of other things you might imagine a woman would appreciate.

Let's suppose for a moment that Dr. Bruin had spoken straightforwardly about the disease. In that case, he would have told us that the course of MS is unpredictable. He would have mentioned the possibility of Ben's paralysis progressing inexorably. "Spasms" is another word he would have used. He would have told us about bodily functions—loss of control thereof. What would we have done in that case?

No doubt exactly what we did, because we were in love. We would have said to each other: "But he said it *might* happen, that doesn't mean it *will* happen. And even if it should happen, we'll manage." Or that's what I would have said.

As it did happen, Dr. Bruin said none of the above. He said the opposite. He leaned forward in his chair, he put his elbows on his desk, he went puff-puff on his pipe, he looked us in the eye. Eyes. "In my opinion," he said in his deeply reassuring European accent, "the disease has burned itself out. It will not progress further."

Wow! Burned out. No further progression. We were so happy we got married right away.

"Let's call him Philip," Ben said.

"*Philip?* Here, *Philip?* Sit, *Philip?*"

"Harry?"

We were lying in bed watching Philip, or Harry, chase his too-long tail.

Yes. He was Harry. And this was a Sunday morning in the cold spring of 1981. We were in northern Massachusetts, where we had gone to visit friends. The dog question had been decided: the person who wants something more than the person who doesn't want it wins. Anyway, it had rained all of Saturday. What was there to do in the country on a rainy day? We checked the local paper for inspiration. At Ben's suggestion, we read the classifieds. So many ads offering puppies! For example: "Adorable black-and-white puppy for adoption."

Our hostess and I took a drive. In an hour or so, we had exhausted the puppy population in the environs of Amherst; dozens of short-haired, brown, houndish mutts yipped and scrambled around muddy yards. Then we drove to a town called Florence, where we inspected the adorable black-and-white puppy. He was indoors, which gave him the advantage of cleanliness. His mother happened to be at home. I must say, she was the oddest-looking dog I ever saw, with a big brown wiry head on a sausage-shaped, short-legged body. Harry did not resemble her in the least. He was mostly black, with a white muzzle, white chest and paws, and white on the tip of his tail; he had rough, shaggy fur that made a fringe over his eyes. Definitely some kind of terrier mix. Three months old, and already he'd been touched by tragedy: someone had adopted him, kept him for a week, and returned him. Poor little puppy. He let me pet him, he wagged his tail and licked my hand. I melted. "He's the one," I said, and didn't think to ask why he'd been returned.

The sweet puppy who slept on my lap during the long drive home was a wild dog. He wouldn't sit and he wouldn't stay. He tore up cushions, he gnawed on books. If I came between him and his food, he growled at me. The aggressive little monster picked dogfights and worked himself into a killing rage. We had him fixed, which helped, but he had to be locked away when infants and small children appeared. I'm sure he thought of them as vermin, because terriers, as I learned too late, are bred specifically to destroy vermin around the farm. They are bred to do this job as independent agents, without reference to human instruction.

We needed help, and that was when we found Phyllis, who trained Harry to sit and stay so well that he became the demo dog in her training classes. When she brought him back to us, he was the same old Harry. This was sometimes humiliating, as when Phyllis brought him home from a training class when we had guests.

"Harry, sit!" I said, wanting to show him off. Nothing.

Sometimes I loved Harry, sometimes I hated him.

When I loved him, I called him pet names, such as Roddy

McDowall, not because I foresaw his eventual show-business connection but because of his eyes, which were just like Roddy McDowall's big, brown human eyes behind the ape mask in *Planet of the Apes*. Sometimes I murmured to Harry, "Are you my beastly boy?" This was love too. When I hated him, I called him "this dog."

"This dog is a nightmare," I'd say to Ben. "He's ruining my life." Honestly? Sometimes I wasn't sure if it was Harry I meant.

Pace Dr. Bruin, in time we were forced to seek other medical opinions. "Burned out?" said Dr. Smith. "Who ever told you such a thing?" This was not a disease that burned out. If you were lucky, you could live a lifetime with mild symptoms—oh, you might become fatigued easily; you might experience temporary periods of weakness in your legs or arms; your vision might grow blurred from time to time.

Ben got unlucky, we got unlucky. This disease was a slow train on a one-way track, traveling from the soles of Ben's feet to the tops of his shoulders. First it finished the job on his legs; it rested for a while at his midsection, the better to do a thorough job deactivating organ reflexes; then it moved up to disable his arms.

If you can believe it, things might have been worse: MS could have paralyzed Ben's swallowing reflex, and that would have been curtains; if it had paralyzed the breathing muscles of his diaphragm, that would have been curtains too. Best of all, it spared his brain, although we neglected to give thanks for such favors. After ten years, the facts on the ground, as far as Ben was concerned, were: no more walking, no more going to the movies on impulse, no more writing by hand or typewriter, goodbye to the pleasures of solitary reading, never again to turn over in bed—just for the sake of turning, mind you, not necessarily to put his arms around me.

As for me, I was in a state of panic during the early years, as each new symptom appeared and we had to learn how to manage it. Not only the symptom but the complications: infected bedsores, bacterial blood infections. Just as I thought we had things under control, something else went haywire, and we had to learn how to deal with that too. I had to learn to deal with it. Do you wonder that I thought of running away from home? Would you believe me if I said those were good years too?

And Harry? Bad dog that he was, he became our bad dog; no question that we belonged to him, and he to us. He was such an entertaining creature. When we took him to Riverside Park, he immediately looked around for a soccer game. If one was in progress, he made himself one of the boys. As soon as the ball was in play, he went after it, took it in his forepaws, ran with it, pushing it ahead of him through the south meadow while a half-dozen teenagers chased after him. If there was no soccer game, he'd insert himself into a game of Frisbee. The blimp was his enemy. He heard the motor long before it appeared and menaced the empty sky with his growls. "Uh-oh, a blimp must be coming," we'd say, and as soon as it hovered into sight Harry barked it off. He was a stalker of squirrels, with such a balletic and patient style that the most infirm squirrel could complete his business without hurry before Harry made the rush. Nothing frightened Harry except those toy cars that work by remote control; it must have been the sound of the electronic device, pitched too high for us to hear, that made him put his tail between his legs and run in the opposite direction.

If Ben's life had been filled with dogs, and it surely had been—Corky, Roderick, Chaing, Poppae, Burnham, Root—Harry was the dog of his life. No wonder. That weekend when we drove to Massachusetts and came home with Harry was the last time Ben would ever drive, and Harry was the last dog he would ever walk.

Phyllis took Harry for his early-morning walk. I walked him the rest of the time. Theoretically, he needed only two more walks a day, but very frequently he had diarrhea and dragged me to the park at two or three in the morning. For years the vet treated him for worms; finally, a new vet diagnosed inflammatory bowel disease. But by that time the disease had advanced too far, and treatment did little good. When he was eleven years old, Harry got cancer of the spleen. Just like him to pick such a bad time. My mother and father were in the last stages of their lives, falling down and breaking bones, in and out of hospitals. It seemed that every other day I was rushing sixty miles upstate for one emergency or another.

We had Harry's spleen taken out. After he recovered from the operation, he seemed fine. We were so happy. I ran into the vet in the park one afternoon. "Look at him!" I said. "He's himself again."

"Yes," said the vet. "That's good." She looked at Harry with no expression.

And soon Harry wasn't his old self. He didn't eat. He dragged himself from room to room. At night, on his pillow beside Ben's bed, he whimpered, and Ben tried to talk him through the night. In the afternoon, when I came home, he could barely wag his tail.

My father died one day in early March. This was 1992. A week later, I was upstate with my mother when Ben called.

"Harry's hemorrhaging," he said. "Phyllis is taking him to the vet."

An hour later, Ben called again. "They want to put him down." He was crying.

Phyllis called. "Should I let them?"

I called Ben. "Should we let them?"

"We have to," he said. "Oh my God, I wish I could be with him."

I wished Ben could be with me.

It wasn't too many months later that my mother died. I missed her by two hours.

Wasn't that a bad time?

For months and months afterward, I dreamed about my mother every night, and Ben dreamed about Harry. One afternoon when he woke up from a nap, he told me he'd dreamed a poem. I wrote it down:

I was a bad dog and didn't obey
any command, until today.

He dreamed the title too. "Stay."

Strangers in the House

You simply can't get good help anymore.

I say this as a woman required to do so. Not that I was raised for such: never in her life did my mother have so much as a weekly cleaning lady, and this was a matter of principle as much as money. For me, in my previous life, it was money, although during a briefly prosperous period, I hired a woman named Divine Love. Later, I married into illness, for which help is a necessity if you're lucky enough to afford it.

In our early days, our honeymoon days, we had Bertha. Bertha came five days a week to do the housework and look after Ben. Ben's MS wasn't very advanced. He could do pretty much everything. He walked, he typed, he cooked, he made love. But his legs weren't working so well. Sometimes he fell. One day, pumped up on steroids, he ran down the subway steps and broke a leg. He began to use a cane, then two canes, a walker. Eventually, he sat down on a little scooter, and after that he didn't get up anymore.

At some point I noticed that Bertha was drinking. When she was drunk, she muttered darkly.

"Bertha," I'd say, "you're drunk."

"Not drunk!"

"Bertha, I smell it!"

"Jess a lil' beer to relax me," she'd say. And then she'd telephone my friend Jenny to complain about being abused by me.

"Bertha," I said, "I think it's time for you to retire." We gave Bertha a huge amount of money and Linda came to keep the house. A year or two after that, Ben's arms became useless. That was the big change, because then he needed more help than I could give. So we hired Alva, and for weekends Ninetta.

I will say nothing here of various transitory helpers: of Lola, who threatened to bash me with an uplifted chair; of Pauline, who borrowed $1,500 on the strength of an eviction notice and immediately disappeared. No, our essential and stable cast for a long time was Linda, who came to clean the house and do laundry a couple of days a week; Alva, who lived with us on weekdays to take care of Ben; and Ninetta, who took Alva's place on weekends.

One day in 1991, B arrived for a job interview with Ben. (Our lawyer says I should not name her, but I feel somehow compelled to reveal that her real name is A.) When B entered our apartment, this was what she saw: in a large, sunny room—our living room—a darkly handsome man, his beard streaked with white, seated in a large electronic wheelchair. Ben did not rise at B's entrance, he did not extend his hand, so B would have quickly gathered that he was paralyzed except for his head and shoulders.

Ben would have seen a young woman. Slim, blond, angular. Not a beauty. (Her mouth was too thin, her eyes were too close-set, her long chin had a definite upward curve.) But she was attractive enough, crisp and clean: her hair was glossy, her clothes pressed, her pale skin without blemish. In her soft voice (I give her that, in the interest of complete disclosure), she would have told Ben that she had literary interests. This would have been important, since she was speaking to a published author and an editor who had founded a celebrated literary magazine. But B's real ambition was to make documentary films. She would not have stressed the fact that she had not yet made any, and that, as she was thirty-three and time was getting on, this was a little worrying.

The job on offer was to come to our house for four hours every weekday, to take Ben's dictation on the computer, to keep the office in order, to be generally pleasant and helpful. B was not exactly in the category of domestic help: her status in the household was more that of a governess than of an upstairs maid. But she was help, and she was in the house.

There is always a first time—the first cigarette before it becomes a habit, the first murder before it becomes thrillingly serial. I'm not sure of the date, but all the evidence indicates that the first time B stole money from Ben was early in 1994. That means Ben had had three years to develop trust in B. To see himself as her mentor, a role he relishes, particularly with young women. And perhaps this time it was something more. I'm sure that B knew exactly how Ben felt. I suspect she may have had a slightly different view of their relationship.

Let's say that on a day in 1994, B looked in her wallet and realized that she was low on cash. But perhaps she already had a plan, and with the plan a theory to justify it. That interests me. Among college-educated middle-class girls, wanting money isn't justification enough for stealing it. It needs rationalization. What was B's?

At that moment in 1994, B finds herself alone in the office. Very casually, she gets up from her desk and strolls down the short corridor leading to the bedroom. So far, there is no one in sight. She makes a left turn into a bright, pleasant room. The walls are crowded with pictures and books, the windows face south to the Hudson. There is a hospital bed, but also some nice furniture, including a pretty red-painted bureau centered on the west wall of the bedroom. As B well knows, Ben's wallet is in the top drawer of the bureau. She opens the bureau drawer, takes out the wallet, and removes some cash. (How much was it that first time?) She slips the money into the back pocket of her jeans and strolls from the room.

But here's a stunner! When B enters the bedroom, she sees Linda, making the bed. Surely at that moment B is startled. Wouldn't you, wouldn't I, turn back? Say something like "Oh. Linda. I was just looking for Ben's glasses." But as we have seen, that didn't happen. And as it turns out, B's gamble pays off. Linda sees B take the money, and she says nothing, not to B, not to Ben, not to me.

Why not? Much later, I asked Linda this question. Her answer was something to the effect of: "I'm just the housekeeper from the jungles of Brazil. B is a white girl, the boss's secretary; he must have said it was okay to take the money. Anyway, I'm not going to make trouble; I could lose my job." And B, who was otherwise so vocal in her sympathies with the peoples of the developing world, so strictly politically correct, depended for her protection on this class difference. Or so I imagine.

Let's give B the benefit of the doubt this one time: let's say that on this occasion, she was repaying herself for an item she had bought for Ben.

But cash continues to inexplicably disappear. Ben says to B, "I know I had more money in my wallet. And what's happening to the office cash?"

B shrugs. I wonder: is there a veiled suggestion in that shrug, and perhaps in a raised eyebrow? Does she intend Ben to infer that Linda is taking it, that Alva is taking it, that I am taking it?

"Well, let's stash it in a book," says my husband.

Without batting an eye, cool as a cucumber, butter wouldn't melt in her mouth, B chooses the book—a volume of art history, I believe—in which to hide the cash. And still cash is disappearing. Wouldn't you think the man would get a glimmer?

But no. Ben, a man of enthusiasms, is B's enthusiast. "How intelligent B is," my husband tells me, "how varied and deep her interests; this film she wants to make, I'd like to help her." At some point he begins to refer to B as his partner.

Do you see what's going on here? Because I didn't.

As for Linda, she may not have told us what she saw in the bedroom that day, but she has told Alva. They're from the same country, they speak the same language, they're friends; of course she told Alva. What wonderful gossip! What human interest! And power! They know something we don't know. From now on they keep their eyes open and notice how often a certain large red volume of art history is taken from the shelf.

"B, could you come in here?" Linda hears Ben call from the living room.

"I'll be right there," B replies, and Alva or Linda watch as B coolly replaces a big red book on the shelf and sticks some cash into her knapsack.

Alva is a strange one. A tiny woman, probably in her late thirties when she came to us. Cute: like a cross between a cat and a lemur. I spent weeks teaching her how to take care of Ben. To wash him, dress him, get him up from bed with the mechanical lift, help him into his chair.

At first she has no English at all, and I mistake her silence for serenity. As she learns the language, she turns into a chatterer. She intimates that she once had a husband—or is it a lover?—who did her wrong. Somebody did her wrong. She hints that once upon a time, wealth was her portion, and a grander style of life. I sense bitterness and volatility: she professes love for me, for Ben, but after a while she loves only our dog, Daisy.

Oh, how she loves our little black Daisy!

"Daisy is my happiness," she tells me. "You believe?"

"I believe."

And then she tells me about the trustworthiness of animals in contrast to the people who have dared to cross her. All those people—they lived to regret the advantage they took of Alva: she has taken her revenge on them.

This is all a bit worrying to me. But Alva is so competent, she takes such good care of Ben, that I want her to stay. To tell the truth, I don't want to take the time and trouble to train someone else. So I listen to all her stories, I offer advice, I soothe her, I agree with her. I can't seem to achieve the civil but distant manner appropriate to an employer. Friendliness, or its appearance, is the best I can do.

Inevitably, one day about five years into our "friendship," Alva turns on me.

What did I do? What did I say? Did I make the mistake of praising Ninetta, who is her weekend rival? Did I inadvertently miscount her salary and leave out a twenty-dollar bill?

It starts one evening after dinner. We are in the kitchen, loading the dishwasher.

"You think I love you," Alva says. "You think everybody loves you. Nobody likes you. They talk about you behind your back. They tell me what they really think."

What is she talking about? Why is she yelling at me? And who are these people telling her what they really think of me? Linda? Ninetta? B? Come to think of it, I have noticed a certain coziness between Alva and B: much tea drinking in the kitchen, Alva chattering, B listening.

For a month Alva heaps angry contempt on me. Sometimes I feel I've been hijacked into that movie where Dirk Bogarde reduces his employer to sniveling slavery. At last I've had enough. One day I say, "Alva, I don't want to come home every day to someone who hates me. You have to leave." I give her four weeks' notice.

Ninetta, who has been working weekends, will take Alva's weekday job. Alva has trained her, and she is a little frightened of Alva, as I now am myself. Still, they have become friendly enough so that Alva has confided in Ninetta what she and Linda know. Now three of our employees are keeping B's secret. Four, if you count B.

But Ninetta hates B. As she sees it, B not only usurps Ben's affections, which rightfully should be hers, but she gets his money. B works, what? Four hours a day, and most of the time she comes late. She sweet-talks Ben, then rolls her eyes behind his back. She spends hours on the phone with her friends. She leaves her used cups and dishes around the house for someone else to pick up.

This is intolerable to Ninetta, who works her ass off. Ninetta is as fierce as a pit bull, or a Sicilian on a quest for *giustizia*.

"You know what goes on in this house, Dorothy," Ninetta says to me. It's not a question.

"What do you mean, Ninetta?"

"You know. You know."

No, how would I know? No one tells me anything. Cryptic hints in pidgin English are all I get.

Ninetta watches B constantly. She's on her like white on rice. Ninetta notes the pilfering of cash, but she's noticed something else. The checkbook.

"You think you are queen in this house," Ninetta says to me. "You are not the queen."

"Who is queen, Ninetta? You?"

"No, I am not. You know who is."

No. I know nothing. But I must say that something is making me uneasy.

"Ben," I say, "Linda says she doesn't work for B. So please ask B to put her leftover food in the garbage and her dishes in the dishwasher."

"Ben," I say, "the office is a mess. Books and papers are piling up on every surface. Why isn't B filing this stuff?"

"Ben," I say, "B always comes late. It interferes with everyone's routine."

Mind you, I am not at home during most of B's tour, but when I come home, I notice that she is always talking and laughing softly into the phone, clearly not on Ben's business. I notice that she reads magazines in the pauses between Ben's dictation, and that she seems irritated when he begins to dictate again. And here's something that really riles me: when B uses the last of the toilet paper in my bathroom, she doesn't replace it. Not just once does she neglect to replace it, not just twice. She *never* replaces it! How often have I reached back to find an empty cardboard roll? It's a small thing, right? But when it's a regular thing, rather aggressive in a passive way, no?

"Ben," I say, "please ask her to replace the toilet paper, do the filing, clean up her messes."

Ben says, "We're working on a documentary. I'm going to produce it."

Well. You tell me what it means to be a producer. My understanding is that it means providing the money.

"Are you giving B the money for this movie?"

"Some of it," he says.

I suspect that he is underreporting.

This is a facer.

And by what right do I interfere?

Because you could drown in Ben's needs, and I am trying to stay afloat. Can you imagine how enormous his needs are, how engulfing? His mind is whole, and he needs the whole of life—friends, work, travel, movies, love, sex. For nine years he ran a literary magazine (with a staff of beautiful girls, I might add; none stole a penny, though I suspect that one or two briefly stole his heart). He wrote a brilliant memoir, but now his energy is sinking, and although he still writes, the pieces are short and take a long time to complete. Once a passionate reader, he can no longer turn the pages of a book; once a world traveler, he now has trouble getting on a local bus. Not to speak of turning on a light switch or turning on the television set, making a phone call, rolling over in bed, feeding himself.

In the years before total paralysis set in, we were almost like normal people. We drove to Massachusetts to stay with friends; we flew to Colorado for Ben's daughter's graduation; we rented a house on Long Island for a few weeks; we went to the movies and the theater, restaurants.

We couldn't keep it up, not without an entourage of help that we couldn't afford. With the increasing paralysis, the bladder and bowel problems, and the spasms that came with it all, I began to say, "No, we can't go, it's too hard for me." We still laughed a lot, but all forms of physical fun went out the window.

So that was where we were when B came along. My husband, his life increasingly locked in, and every day when I am off working, B is offering Ben a life. Sometimes they go to movies together, to museums. Incidentally, doesn't he love films? Why not underwrite her project? To what extent? To the extent of the budget she presents to him. Is the budget inflated? I'd bet the house on it! In return for all this money, in return for access to Ben's friends who can help her, Ben gets B's companionship and a big credit as producer. In this way, thousands of dollars are transferred to B. Legitimately. And, by the way, Ben is happy.

I didn't interfere. I had no right.

· · ·

"So, Alva," I say cheerfully. "This is your last day with us."

Alva screams. She falls to the floor, writhing. Her arms and legs jerk and flail. A seizure? I call for B and hold Alva's jerking arms while B forces a spoon into her mouth. B is bending over Alva, and I am calling 911, when I hear Alva whisper to B, "Don't leave me alone with Dorothy, she'll kill me."

The EMS technician takes a look at the "fit" and puts a bag over Alva's face: hyperventilation. She has worked herself into this state. Nevertheless, they take her to the emergency room. I cannot leave Ben; B goes with her. That night Ben says to me, "You ought to talk to B. Tell her about your troubles with Alva."

"B," I say the next day, "I'm really grateful that you took Alva to the hospital. I'd like to tell you why I fired her."

B is sitting at her desk reading. She doesn't look up. "I don't want to hear it," she says.

Now *this* is odd. Hostile, actually. I think about all those times I reached for the toilet paper to find an empty roll. I think about the cozy tea parties in the kitchen, B and Alva chatting away. All those hours B has spent with Alva, no doubt listening to tales of my egregious nature.

"B was distinctly unfriendly to me," I say to Ben. "I'm taking offense. You should too."

How could I have imagined the next step in this drama?

"Alva is going to sue you," Linda says to me.

"What for?"

"She's going to say that she hurt her wrist working here. Also that you were paying her off the books."

"Oh, please," I say. "She's got no case."

"Listen to me," Linda says. "B is helping her."

"What do you mean?"

"Just believe me. Don't say anything in front of B that you don't want Alva to know. B will tell her. B went with Alva to a lawyer to give a deposition against you."

"I don't believe it."

"I'm telling you. Also, Alva asked me to kidnap Daisy."

What is going on here? Just in case Linda is not paranoid, I write out a long statement to our lawyer. I describe Alva's five years of employment with us and the reasons I fired her. I fax the statement. Stupidly, stupidly, because I cannot fathom such betrayal, I leave the original statement next to the fax machine. The next day, when I look for it, it's gone.

"That paper you sent to your lawyer?" Linda says. "B took it. She gave it to Alva. Alva gave it to her lawyer."

I tell Ben. He doesn't believe it, I can't believe it, we ignore it. B continues her work as usual. And remember: we still don't know about the money. And even if we had known, we wouldn't have known the half of it.

What I think now is that B's relationship with Alva was, in part, an alliance of necessity on B's part. Alva knew about the money. But B was also a girl who liked to be in the right: to hold correct political and moral positions. The badly mistreated third-world Alva—exploited and abused, as she would have insisted—must have been balm to B's conscience. Yes, wasn't she, B, making a political statement by exploiting the exploiter? Even apart from that, Ben was so generous, he cared so much for B, wouldn't he have wanted her to have what she needed?

But really, I'm grasping at straws here.

• • •

Now it's 1999. One evening Ninetta says, "Dorothy, come to the kitchen. I want to show you something."

We sit at the kitchen table. Ninetta hands me the office checkbook. "Look. Count. How many times she pays herself her salary?"

B has had free access to the office checkbook: she pays the office bills. She affixes Ben's signature with the stamp authorized by the bank. She writes the checks for her salary.

The checkbook Ninetta gives me goes back only one year. I begin to count. How many weeks were there last year? Seventy-two? Because that's how many salary checks B wrote to herself. Instead of four checks a month, there are often six, each made out for the exact amount of her salary. And when her two-week vacation rolls around, she pays herself for four weeks.

A checkbook is like a novel. I read in it the day B's salary was raised by $100 a week. That was a year earlier.

In 1998, B asked Ben for a raise. A hundred dollars a week, please.

"You know I can't afford that," Ben said. "I have to cut expenses; money is just pouring out. I don't understand it. At this rate, I won't have enough to go on working very much longer."

B burst into tears.

"I'll give you fifty," Ben said.

And still B wept. Really she did, as though she had forgotten that her tricks with the checkbook and the wallet had already raised her salary by quite a bit, perhaps by enough so that she and her boyfriend could afford the lovely new apartment they moved into. She had been embezzling for so long without being caught that she may have believed she was entitled to every check she wrote to herself. So just last year, with Ben, she wept and sincerely pleaded for her well-deserved raise until he gave in.

As she continued to write her own checks for her salary, each one included her $100 raise, as did each of the unauthorized salary checks. Nothing fancy about her method of embezzlement; it was simple and effective as long as no one was counting.

I went to the basement where the canceled checks were stored. I rooted through everything in that dusty, dirty storeroom. I took it all to the accountant.

"Anything amiss here?" I asked the accountant, who had not been counting either.

So, over a five-year period starting in 1994, B wrote herself checks amounting to about $40,000 above her salary. We'll never know how much cash she took. And this was in addition to the thousands Ben voluntarily handed over for her art's sake. What this amount signifies—no secret to B, who knew exactly the condition of Ben's finances—is that there will come a time, two or three years earlier than it should have, when Ben can no longer afford to pay an assistant, and therefore, when he can no longer write, no longer keep up correspondence, he will no longer keep a place in the world.

Ben is devastated, humiliated, heartbroken. He telephones B. "Is this true?" he asks.

B bursts into tears. "Oh," she sobs, "I'm so bad with money."

Well put, wouldn't you say?

Oh my goodness, the themes you stumble over as you make your way from day to day! Trust, Betrayal, Class, Hypocrisy, Love, Hate, Greed, Sickness, Health. It only needs War and Peace.

Somewhere in all this, there must be a lesson. Is it: don't get cozy with the help? Is it that household politics are simply politics writ small? Is it that greed and betrayal lurk like bacteria awaiting a failure of the immune system? Is it that one should always use a bonded employment agency? Is it life, or what?

Dumb Luck

> What . . .
> If I'd been born
> in the wrong tribe,
> with all roads closed before me?
>
> —WISŁAWA SZYMBORSKA

Liya Alexandrovna Gordeeva is my first cousin once removed. Some people are confused by the once-removed relationship, but it's really very simple. The removal takes place parallel with generations: the child of my mother's sister (or brother) is my first cousin; the child of this first cousin is my first cousin once removed; if my once-removed cousin should have a child, it will be my first cousin twice removed. I won't get into the second- and third-cousin business.

I could simply have said that Liya Alexandrovna is my

cousin and let it go at that, but I wanted to make the point that Liya is not a close relative. Not only that, she was born in Moscow and has never left that city. Until last summer, I had never been to Moscow and so had never laid eyes on her.

I did know that she existed. I knew that she was the daughter of my mother's niece, Betya. I knew that (things being what they were in the Soviet Union) my mother and her sisters had regularly sent money to Betya. I knew that Betya had a daughter named Liya and that the two of them had always lived together, much to Betya's dismay. When Betya died, which was sometime in the late eighties, my mother and her sisters continued to send money to Liya.

The long and the short of it is that the time came when my cousins and I inherited Liya. We took it for granted that we were obligated to send her money, as our mothers had done, and we knew that except for us, Liya was all alone: no husband, no children, no other relatives, no job. We had the impression that she somehow wasn't equipped to make her way in the world.

It didn't seem so onerous a burden to take responsibility for one person in the world among the millions in need. We chipped in; every third month, I wired three hundred dollars to Moscow and didn't think of Liya Alexandrovna until the next time this act of filial piety was due.

Things went on in this way for a number of years. We sent the money, Liya collected it. And then she didn't. A year's worth of money piled up in the Western Union office in Moscow. What to do? Maybe Liya had died. We located an agency that catered to Moscow's Jewish population, and pretty soon I got an e-mail from a social worker:

Dear Dorothy,

I visited your cousin Liya Alexandrovna Gordeeva in her apartment in Moscow on November 16, 2004. I was able to talk to Ms. Gordeeva and enter her apartment with the assistance of Liya's neighbor. Normally, Liya doesn't allow strangers into her apartment.

Liya looked unkempt, untidy (a torn housedress, uncombed hair, torn slippers, clearly in need of a bath). The apartment was stuffy and dusty. There is a broken bed in one of the rooms. There is a big crack along the kitchen wall. There are cockroaches in the kitchen. There is no refrigerator, no washer. Her phone has been disconnected for nonpayment.

Liya receives a pension of 2,383 roubles a month ($90). She pays 950 roubles for the utilities and apartment maintenance, and about 260 roubles for medications for her heart. She eats one meal a day. Typically she has oatmeal, or macaroni and tea. There's a grocery close by where she could go herself, but she doesn't go because she cannot afford anything. She said that her U.S. relatives used to send her money but she got sick and couldn't pick up the money transfers. When she finally got to the bank it was too late, and the bank refused to give it to her.

Liya refused any assistance or services. She says that she can clean the house herself, but she doesn't feel like doing so. She is also very frightened to go any distance from her apartment . . .

Oh. *This* was my once-removed cousin. Suddenly real in torn housecoat and slippers. I could see her shuffling around that apartment. I could see the cockroaches scuttling in the kitchen, the crack in the wall. I could feel the depression and loneliness that kept her from cleaning house. I could imagine that when she woke up every morning, a hot cup of tea was her only comfort in the long hours of nothing to do, no one to see, one paltry meal to mark the end of another day. I thought about the year Liya had been born, 1944, and what it meant to be born in Moscow during the war. I thought of Liya's mother, Betya, of Betya's mother, Rivka, who was my own mother's sister, and what it had meant to those three women to live their lives in that benighted country from which most of their family had the luck to escape.

On my way to Moscow last September, I stopped off in the Ukraine. Since I was going in that direction anyway, I wanted to take a look at my mother's hometown. The town is called Murafa, and it is a *very* small town, not even a dot on most maps. If, by some chance, you want to locate it, find Kiev on the map, then move your finger southwest about an inch, where you should find the city of Vinnitsya; continue on that line for less than an eighth of an inch. Unless you have a large-scale map, you won't find the name, Murafa, but that's where it is. Or, if you should ever find yourself in the town of Shargorod, drive past the statue of Lenin in the center of town, continue east on that road for seven kilometers, through hilly, wild countryside, then bear left after the hammer-and-sickle monument that to this day marks the road into Murafa.

The first thing you will see, should you drive into town, is a Roman Catholic cathedral, built by a Polish count in the eighteen hundreds; then an Orthodox church, both looming on the town's unpaved, dusty main street. My mother saw those churches every day, as well as the hilly green landscape and the houses, hidden for the most part down dirt lanes behind overgrown brush and tiny garden plots. I'd never seen such defiantly undecorated houses: no carved wood, no paint, no pleasure for the eye, each house an assertion that shelter is the best you can hope for.

Just a few steps from the town, the old Jewish cemetery still exists. It was vandalized during the war but, miraculously, not destroyed. Hundreds and hundreds of age-blackened head-stones, the oldest dated 1638, roll with the landscape across a grassy plateau that drops sharply away to fields below. The inscriptions on the stones are too faint to make out, even for someone who can read Hebrew, which I cannot. But the carv-ings are still distinct—a pair of praying hands indicates that a priestly Cohen is buried beneath; a bird in flight memorializes a woman named Faigle, which means "bird"; a water pitcher for a Levi. In one section of the cemetery, a grove of apple trees drop perfect fruit between the stones.

But at the center of town, where the open market was once held, where the Jewish houses clustered, where the Jewish shops were built, where Jewish trades were practiced, where three syn-agogues stood, nothing. A rubble-strewn space overgrown with weeds. Dead ground.

My grandfather kept a shop here. My grandmother, begin-ning her labors before the turn of the last century, gave birth to nine children here. One of her sons died of scarlet fever when he was five or six years old, and his bones probably lie in the Jew-ish cemetery. Of the other children, seven made it to America, where they lived long lives and died of nothing more serious than disease, one fluke accident, and old age. Only Rivka, the first of my grandmother's children, my mother's eldest sister, was left behind.

• • •

Rivka Rendar married Aron Vaks in Murafa. I have a picture taken on their wedding day. There are three people in the photograph. Rivka, seated on a bentwood chair in the photographer's studio, a pretty, pale girl, her face still rounded with baby fat. She is dressed in white. A ruffle is at her throat, a flounce decorates her sleeves, a locket is hung around her neck. I can just make out a white shoe beneath the hem of her dress. Her left elbow is propped on the tasseled arm of the chair, her chin rests on her hand. She leans toward her mother, my grandmother, who is seated next to her. It seems to me that my grandmother looks a little dispirited, considering the occasion, and neither is the bride smiling. Standing behind the two women is the new husband, Aron, a dark, thin, serious-looking boy wearing a three-piece suit, with a watch chain draped across his waistcoat.

I see that Rivka's hair is light, no doubt the same shade of reddish-blond that turns up in my family now and then. Her face is the original version of her sisters' faces, which are as familiar to me as my own. Aron seems delicate, definitely not robust. My grandmother may already suspect that he will not be a good earner, which may account for her grim expression.

The date of this marriage is not recorded, but I can make an educated guess. I figure that it is late 1913, or early the following year, because in 1915 Rivka will give birth to her daughter, Betya. I'm pretty sure that the wedding took place in Murafa, which is not only Rivka's hometown but probably Aron's as well. I say this because Vaks—Aron's family name—is written in the Murafa town register for the year 1945.

"Aren't there any earlier records?" I asked the mayor of Murafa.

"No," he said. "Everything was destroyed during the war."

I pointed to a word that followed all the Jewish names in the register. "What does this mean?"

"It means 'left,' " he said. "They all left."

I can tell you this much: the Ukrainian countryside is beautiful, and it reminds me of Iowa or Idaho. In mid-September, when the harvest is in, flocks of crows and geese settle on the rich black soil to glean the leavings. Murafa itself is as strange and other-worldly to me as those crossroads in the middle of the American nowhere that serve as towns for Indian reservations—a few shabby buildings in an empty countryside, under a dwarfing sky. I am helpless to imagine the life that was lived here. And is lived here still, except that there are no Jews anymore. I see that old women sit all day by the side of the road, minding a single cow as it grazes. As we drive through the country, I see that it is studded with plaques memorializing the massacres of World War II: BOW YOUR HEAD PASSERBY . . . At a railroad station, where freight cars stand on the sidings, a notice: FROM HERE 500,000 JEWS WERE SENT TO BERDICHEV . . . In Kiev, near the beautiful cathedral of Santa Sophia, I saw a huge monumental bronze statue of a man seated on a rearing horse.

Who is that? I ask. Why, that's Bohdan Khmelnytsky, a seventeenth-century hero of Ukrainian history. In his quest to liberate the Ukraine from Poles and their agents, the Jews, his Cossacks killed hundreds and thousands of them, impaling some alive on wooden stakes.

And one day, in Murafa, my aunt Rivka married a local boy, for love or not.

If we assume that the wedding took place early in the spring of 1914, we know that the sky was about to fall. In the space of a historical fraction of a second, World War I would come, the Bolshevik coup would follow, civil war would erupt; famine was around the corner. My grandfather was not so prescient, but he knew the present and the past. He knew that he lived in a place where Jews were an untouchable, despised caste. Almost everything had been forbidden to them: to move outside the Pale of Settlement, even to travel inside it without a permit; to own land, to go to school, except by minuscule quota. Jews were blamed for everything. For the assassination of Czar Alexander II. For the ritual murder of Christian children so as to obtain Christian blood to bake in their matzos.

"Nine-tenths of the troublemakers are Jews, and the people's whole anger turned against them . . . That's how the pogrom happened," Czar Nicholas wrote to his mother. He was referring to the six-hundred-odd pogroms that took place in the failed revolutionary year of 1905, when more than three thousand Jews were murdered. Once upon a time, it was common practice for Ukrainians to hang a Pole, a Jew, and a dog from the same tree. If this was a recreation peculiar to the seventeenth century, its spirit remained. You could never tell when the moment would come again.

In the early years of the twentieth century, Jews are leaving the country in droves, and my grandfather, too, has made his decision. One by one he is sending his children away. By the time Rivka married, three of his children, my mother included, were already in America. My grandfather intends the rest of the family to follow soon, and for our centuries-long sojourn in the Ukraine to come to an end.

Centuries-long? I don't know. There have been Jews in this part of the world for over a thousand years, wandering in from the east, the south, and the west as they were expelled elsewhere for the crime of being Jewish. Why, this place has hardly ever been a country at all. Its very name has been an invitation to hordes of murderous invaders: "Ukraine" means "no particular place," means "border-land." However long my family has lived here, it is long enough.

During World War I, half a million looting German and Aus-trian troops invaded the Ukraine. The war's end in 1918 scarcely made a difference. The Bolshevik coup brought ragtag Red and White armies, plus invading Poles, fighting a savage civil war, looting and raping their way through the towns and villages of the Ukraine. I don't have to imagine this. I need only open Isaac Babel's 1920 diary to the first entry. Here is Babel, riding with the Red Cavalry of Cossack troops. On June 3, they stop in the Ukrainian town of Zhitomir:

> *Zhitomir pogrom, organized by the Poles, continued, of course, by the Cossacks . . .*
>
> *Poles entered the town, stayed for 3 days, there was a pogrom, they cut off beards, that's usual, assembled 45 Jews in the marketplace, led to them to the slaughter yard, tortures, cut out tongues, wails heard all over the square. They set fire to 6 houses . . . machinegunned those who tried to rescue people. The yardman into whose arms a mother dropped a child from a burning building was bayoneted . . .*
>
> *The faces of the old Jews.*

On July 11:

Same old story, the Jews have been plundered, their
bewilderment, they expected the Soviet regime to liberate them
and suddenly there were shrieks, whips, cracking, shouts of
"dirty Yid."

One day a pogrom broke out in Murafa. Everyone fled the house in panic, abandoning four-year-old Betya. I think of my aunt Frieda, then fourteen or fifteen years old, who ran back to get the baby.

I think of my grandfather's shop. What did he sell—dry goods? Flour and salt? Syrups? His shop would have been looted, all his stock confiscated. How did they survive, my grandparents who had four young children at home, plus a married daughter, her husband, a grandchild? This would have been the time to flee the country, but there was no getting out now: the international borders were sealed.

I think it was in 1920 when my family, the Rendars, together with Rivka and her family, the Vaks, left Murafa for a town called Mogilev Podolski. They may have fled willy-nilly, from fear and panic, and hunger, for famine swept the Ukraine during the war years 1920–21. Here on my desk is another photograph of Rivka and her family taken in Mogilev, five or six years after her wedding picture. She scarcely looks like the same person. Hunger has sculpted her face, and she is all gaunt cheekbones and staring eyes. Aron is sunken in his chair, and most of his hair is gone. Two children are with them now: Betya, five or six years old, sullenly standing beside Rivka, with her hand in her mother's lap. Aron holds their son, a boy, Yefim. The woman standing behind them may be Aron's sister, and perhaps they fled to Mogilev because she offered to take them in.

But Mogilev may have been a more deliberate choice since it has the distinct advantage of being closer to an escape route. A moment came in the confusion of the civil war when my grandfather found a boatman willing to smuggle the family across the Dniester River into Moldova. From Moldova, they made their way to Bucharest, where the older girls, Frieda and Rachile, got factory jobs to support the family. Everyone waited—a year, even two—until the children in America could send for them. In the records of immigrants processed through Ellis Island, I find that Max and Chaika Rendar, together with four minor children—Frieda, Rachile, Iosif, and little Berka— were allowed to pass through the portals in 1922.

In fact, not all four children were minors: Frieda, who was twenty at the time, was passed off as seventeen, and Rachile as fifteen when she was actually eighteen. Rivka and Aron were long past such fudging. Two small children may have been sufficient reason to stay behind. Or maybe they said, "We'll join you later." But it occurs to me that Rivka may have consoled herself for the loss of her family with the Bolshevik promise of emancipation of the Jews. The new Soviet government had outlawed anti-Semitism. The Pale of Settlement had been lifted. Jews could move from their small shtetl towns to larger towns, to cities; they could be educated, join the professions. Jews were prominent in the new regime, they exercised power. In theory, Jews could become Soviets, if not actual Russians.

Rivka remained in close touch with her family after their emigration. Throughout the twenties, the families exchanged news.

Betya was going to school, and she seemed to have a talent for music. Yefim too had entered school, and Aron was as well as could be expected.

For her part, Rifka learned that American streets did not actually run with milk and honey, but little by little, her family was prospering. Her mother and father were still in good health; her sisters and brothers found work, and one by one they were getting married, children were being born: her favorite sister, Frieda, had a son. And everyone was eager for news of the Soviet Union. Was it true that Utopia was being created? A new Soviet Man? Indeed, Rachile, Rivka's youngest sister, was fervent in her belief that it was so. She had joined the American Communist Party, and she talked of returning to Russia.

And so she did. Rachile came in 1929. I suspect that she chose that time because an American delegation of the Communist Party of America was also traveling to Moscow then, to meet with the Comintern. Among the documents Rachile brought with her, and left with Rivka, was her membership card in the Communist Party, which shows that she had become a full-fledged member that year.

Political considerations aside, the reunion between the sisters was surely joyful. Almost a decade had passed since Rachile and Rivka had seen each other. Rachile was in her middle twenties, and a photograph taken at this time shows that she had become a strikingly beautiful woman. Rivka, in her mid-thirties, looks worn but lovely; the hungry look of the early twenties has disappeared. Betya, whom Rachile had taken care of as a small girl, was now a plump fourteen-year-old. Yefim, born after Rachile's emigration, was ten.

Evidently, nothing Rachile saw during her 1929 trip, nothing she heard during that decisive year when Stalin succeeded in ousting Trotsky from the leadership of the Party, discouraged her plan to make a permanent move. But by 1932, when she came back again, with her husband, Victor, planning to stay, events had taken a dreadful turn.

For Rachile, incredulity turned to disillusion. Disillusion went deep and was bitter and lifelong. Back in America, Rachile and Victor tried to describe what they had seen. My mother, for one, refused to believe them, and that rift between the sisters never healed. And what was it they had seen? Not your ordinary famine caused by war or a failure of the harvest. No, the Ukrainian harvest had been perfectly fine that year. This was Stalin's famine, his "revolution from above," the one that required breaking eggs for the omelet. The peasants of the Ukraine, so resistant to Stalin's plan for collectivization of farming, were to be crushed, starved, deported. It began with the requisition of food, all the food, all the seed stock. It proceeded to the point where one Party "activist," charged with the collection of foodstuffs in the Ukraine, wrote to his superior that he could meet the quota for meat, but it would have to be with human flesh. Boris Pasternak wrote, "What I saw could not be expressed in words. There was such inhuman, unimaginable misery, such a terrible disaster . . . it would not fit within the bounds of consciousness. I fell ill. For an entire year I could not write."

Starving, bloated bodies lay where they fell—the children, the animals—it was unspeakable. Millions died, but not Rivka and her family. Of course, they couldn't emigrate. No one was allowed out by then. But they survived, as they would survive Stalin's purges of the thirties. No neighbor denounced them as traitors, the midnight knock on the door never came. How did they get so lucky?

• • •

In the early thirties, the Vaks moved from Mogilev to the town of Uman, not too far from Kiev. A year or two later, Betya was sent to study at a teacher training school in Odessa. She spent a year in Odessa and then decided to study music at the conservatory in Kiev. I have her school report, dated 1939. Her photograph is pasted on the cover: at nineteen, her face is rounded with baby fat, like her mother's at that age. She wears her dark hair in a coronet of braids. Her school report describes her as a satisfactory student, passable at languages, good at music. Her instrument was the harp. A famous Russian harpist heard Betya play in Kiev and took her to the conservatory in Moscow for further study. Her brother, Yefim, visited her in Moscow, heard her play in concert, and wrote a poem to her:

> The pen is trembling in my hand . . . you my sweet sister
> you play on the harp with the souls of your fingers
> music has risen to the heavens
> Oh how envious I am of you that the sounds of the strings
>   obey you
> I would give up everything if this favor from god would be
>   given to me . . .

That sort of thing. Sweet, full of genuine feeling if not literary promise. But by that time Yefim wouldn't have had much competition in the literary field. Mandelstam, Babel, Meyerhold, Pilnyak, more than a thousand of Russia's glorious artists, had been arrested and executed. On the night of May 29, 1939, Isaac Babel was interrogated:

*"You have been arrested for treacherous anti-Soviet
activities. Do you acknowledge your guilt?"*

"No, I do not . . ."

"Do not wait until we force you! Begin your confession."

Yefim titled the poem he wrote to his sister "Golden
Sound" and dated it May 1, 1941. Betya's school year had two
more months to run. After that, she planned to spend an indolent
summer with her parents in Uman. It was true that Europe was
at war, that Hitler had marched into Poland, Belgium, and
France. But Russians had nothing to fear. Hadn't Stalin signed a
pact with Hitler? He had shown his good faith by sharing with
Hitler his information on the Polish resistance, so that Hitler
might more easily destroy it. In the name of Nazi-Soviet friendship, Stalin had gone further: he had rounded up, and returned
to Hitler, the thousands of German Communists who had taken
refuge in the Soviet Union. And yet, on June 22, a bare seven
weeks after Yefim wrote his poem, the German army overran the
Ukraine, and Rivka found it necessary to warn Betya: *Do not
come! It's dangerous.*

Mogilev, Murafa, Uman, it made no difference. Almost every
Jew in those towns was either murdered on the spot or marched
to concentration areas to be killed. The Germans came for the
Jews of Uman on September 16. The men were taken away first,
ordered to dig long ditches in front of the airport. Aron was
taken with them. Rivka ran through the streets, screaming in
terror. She wasn't the only woman screaming.

Guards—Germans and their willing helpers, Ukrainians—

were stationed at the airport square and the railroad station to prevent escapes. An order was posted on the streets of Uman: all Jews, of all ages, were to assemble the following morning at the airport to register for a census. Those who failed to appear would be severely punished.

Tables were set up in the square. Jews lined up. But no count was taken. Instead, they were ordered to undress and hand over everything they carried. Clothes and jewelry were placed on the tables. Men and women, mothers carrying babies, stood naked in the dawn light. In front of them were the ditches. Then the screams began again as one line after another was mowed down with automatic pistols. A German lieutenant named Erwin Bingle, stationed in Uman that day, has left us his recollections of this event:

> Nor were the mothers spared the terrible sight of their children being gripped by their little legs and put to death with one stroke of the pistol butt, or club, thereafter to be thrown on the heap of human bodies in the ditch, some of which were not quite dead . . . The people in the first row thus having been killed in the most inhuman manner, those in the second row were ordered to step forward. The men in this row were . . . handed shovels with which to heap chloride of lime upon the still partly moving bodies . . .

Even considering that the work had started at dawn, the numbers are staggering: in only one day, and without special killing equipment, twenty-four thousand Jews were gunned down in Uman on September 16, 1941.

· · ·

Betya did not set foot in Uman until the seventies. She found, to her surprise, that her parents' house was still standing. She knocked on the door. A woman answered.

"Did you know my parents?" Betya asked.

"Oh yes," the woman said. "I knew them when I was a child. I was in the grave. I was saved at the last moment. I saw your mother in there."

Betya was in Moscow through the war years. Yefim went into the army. He was a dreamy, artistic boy, but he fought and survived a number of battles. In 1944 he was fighting in the Crimea; on April 28 he was killed in a battle near Sevastopol.

The Germans were on a direct path to Moscow. On September 19 they occupied Kiev; two weeks later, they drove the Jews of Kiev into a deep natural ravine in the forest at Babi Yar and slaughtered them as they lay. As the Germans moved closer to Moscow, Stalin evacuated the government from the city, though he remained. By late November, two German units were in the Moscow suburbs, within sight of the Kremlin. Imagine the fear and chaos: the government gone from the city; factories, offices, and schools shut down; heating, sanitation, food supplies, the infrastructure of civilized life—all on the verge of collapse, and the Germans in sight. But on November 7, Stalin staged the traditional military parade in Red Square to honor the anniversary of the revolution. Some spectators might have regretted the absence, in this time of war, of the best and finest officers of the Red Army and Navy. Stalin had purged—shot—more than fifty thousand of them between 1937 and 1939. Nevertheless, the spectacle had its intended effect. Moscow rallied. The remainder

of the army mobilized. Citizen volunteer divisions were organized. Women served as nurses for the wounded, and as snipers.
The Russian winter froze the German army, along with their
tanks and equipment, but the bombs kept falling. The Battle of
Moscow cost tens of thousands of lives.

What happened to Betya during the war? At the very least,
Red Cross documents show that between June 1941 and August
of the following year, she gave over five liters of her blood. And
yet, miraculously, in 1942, although there was little food in the
city and no way to keep warm, the music conservatory reopened,
and Betya was lucky enough to get a job playing with the orches-
tra at the Central Children's Theatre.

And there is another photograph: pretty, dark-eyed Betya
stands between two handsome soldiers. She looks happy. She is
in love. On the back of the photo, the soldier she loves has written, TO MY BELOVED BETYA. The date is January 1942. The
soldier's name is Isaac Gershlibersohn. He was born in Kharkov,
had moved to Moscow to study acting, and when war came, he
joined the Red Army. Eventually he was sent to the western
front, where he was killed, fighting in Poland, in October 1944.

It seems to me that I recently read something about that
period of the war. October 1944? Yes. The Warsaw Uprising
had begun in July of that year. The Polish Home Army was desperately fighting the Germans, certain that Allied help would
soon arrive. By mid-September, the Red Army had reached the
eastern bank of the Vistula. The Poles could see them. Help was
in sight. But the Red Army stopped at the river's bank and
camped there, under Stalin's orders, for two months, as the Germans destroyed the Home Army and razed Warsaw. Perhaps this
should not have been a surprise. When, under the terms of his

pact with Hitler, Stalin had occupied eastern Poland in 1939, he had murdered thousands of Polish officers in the Katyn forest. Now, close to the war's end, he wanted no resistance to his plans to take over all of Poland as a Soviet satellite. When the Red Army finally moved into the city in October, all was quiet, except perhaps for a few remaining German snipers, one of whom may have taken a shot at Isaac Gershlibersohn.

This is sheer conjecture, except for the fact that Betya lost her sweetheart in Poland in October 1944, and that she gave birth to his daughter, Liya, in war-torn, starving Moscow that same year.

Of course I knew about the war. Didn't we listen to the war news on the radio every night? Didn't I scrape the silver foil from my father's packs of Pall Malls, smooth the foil carefully into sheets, and bring them to school for the war effort? But did I think the war had anything to do with us? Not really. Did I know how frantically my mother and her sisters searched for Rivka and Betya? Honestly, I didn't know these people existed.

In 1947, two long years after the war had ended, Betya managed to get word out. For a brief moment, it seemed that the family in Russia had once again pulled off the trick of survival.

> Betya, dearest one born to us,
>
>> We read in the Jewish paper that you are looking for us. It's hard to describe how we felt when all hope was already lost that any of you stayed alive. Betya dear, you wrote in the paper that because of the war "we lost contact with all our dear ones." Betya, who are the "we" you speak of? Is it possible

that your parents and brother are still alive? Right away, dear one, send us a letter by airplane, and tell us everything in detail.

We, too, tried very hard to find you. Our cousin wrote from Nikolaev that in Uman they killed everyone. Letters which we sent to Uman came back from organizations that tried to find you.

All of us are waiting to hear from you immediately, to find out about all of you. Grandfather says that you should tell us whatever you need and we will send everything.

This is Frieda. I am writing for everyone, for Rachile, Bella, Leiza, Haskell, Iosif, Berka.

I'm hugging you my dear one.

Soon they knew that only Betya was alive, trying to survive with her child in a devastated city. What I remember of this time, by now the fifties, is orgies of shopping. Daily telephone conversations between one or another or all of the sisters, arranging to meet at Macy's, Klein's, or Orbach's, where they searched for bargains and returned home with huge bundles of clothes that had to be wrapped and shipped to Moscow. Why clothes, not money? Soviet citizens were not allowed to receive money. But clothes, especially warm coats, were currency that Betya could sell or trade.

Betya married. We know that Liya's father died in the war, but the other soldier who appeared in the photograph with them had come back. His name was Alexander Gordeev. He had trained as an actor at the Moscow State Jewish Theater School.

It's odd to think that there was a moment when Jewish culture flourished in Soviet Russia. In the mid-twenties, it seemed that the promise of emancipation would be fulfilled. A theater was established where plays were performed in Yiddish; Jewish poets wrote poems in Yiddish, newspapers and books were published in Yiddish. When the Moscow State Jewish Theater was founded in 1925, many Jewish artists were involved—the painter Marc Chagall, the writer Sholem Aleichem, the poet Peretz Markish, the internationally known actor and director Solomon Mikhoels.

When war came to Soviet Russia, how useful the Jews proved to be. Stalin organized a Jewish Anti-Fascist Committee, with Mikhoels as chairman. From June to December 1943, the committee toured America, Mexico, Canada, and England to spread the word of Nazi atrocities and involve foreign Jews in support of the war. In 1946, Mikhoels was awarded the Stalin Prize for his work during the war.

It all ended soon, and would have ended earlier if not for the war. In 1939 Mikhoels was already being set up for arrest. The interrogation of Isaac Babel in June 1939 brought forth a denunciation:

> I met with Solomon Mikhoels, the head of the Jewish State Theatre. With reason, he considered himself an outstanding actor and was constantly dissatisfied [with] the Soviet repertoire . . . He was extremely disapproving of the plays of Soviet dramatists . . .

Four months later, Babel realized that nothing he said would save him. He took back his forced accusations:

> *I slandered certain people and gave false testimony about my*
> *terrorist activities . . . I fabricated my testimony about S. M.*
> *Eisenstein and S. M. Mikhoels.*

Mikhoels was killed in 1948, surviving Babel by eight years. In 1947, *Pravda* had begun a campaign against "rootless cosmopolitans," "persons without identity," "passportless wanderers." No one doubted which people were meant by these scarcely disguised euphemisms. Editorials in *Pravda* denounced Jews as saboteurs of Russian culture, Zionists without loyalty to the Motherland. Another round of show trials was about to begin, this one aimed at Jews. In the five years before his death in 1953, Stalin had ordered the arrest, interrogation, imprisonment, and death of Jewish intellectuals, artists, scientists, and doctors. First they were put on trial. Presiding officer to defendant Solomon Lozovsky:

> *What kind of Bolshevik are you, if you believe that Jews*
> *in our country, in the USSR, do not have equal rights? That is*
> *slander.*

Jewish theaters and schools were closed, Jewish newspapers were banned, Jews lost their jobs, Alexander Gordeev lost his job. Betya's life as a professional musician was finished. Gordeev eventually found work at a government agency as a photographer. Betya found piecework with a factory that manufactured theatrical props. She worked at home all day, and sometimes all night, gluing envelopes together, making artificial flowers, decorating plastic boxes, making braid for the hats of army officers. She lived off of that and the bundles of coats, and later the cash, that kept coming from America. As for us, our house filled up with artificial flowers and decorative plastic boxes.

In the meantime, Liya grew up and went to school—to music school for several years, then to a regular school. If she was a strange child, anxiety-ridden, fearful, obsessive, clinging to her mother, the circumstances of her life would have been enough to explain it. But Betya had her own idiosyncrasies. She was a woman who took up a lot of psychic space. She was demanding, impatient with Liya, annoyed with her, angry much of the time. Her own life was hard enough. Why couldn't the child keep a job? Why couldn't she concentrate on anything? Why would Liya never leave her be? For a while Liya worked at the Lenin Library, but then she quit or was fired and went from one job to another. She was intelligent, quick-witted, there was no doubt about that. But she was lost. Finally, she stopped working altogether. If there was ever a boyfriend or lover, it came to nothing.

In 1966, Betya and Gordeev divorced, but the family continued to live together in a one-room apartment. There was nowhere else to go. In time, Betya's aunts raised enough money for her to buy a place of her own. She found an apartment in an outer ring of Moscow and moved in with Liya. This is the apartment that Liya cannot bring herself to clean, where the kitchen wall is cracked, where roaches scuttle, where my cousin, now in her early sixties, has lived alone for the last twenty years.

At last I've reached Moscow. Here is my cousin Liya opening the door to the apartment. I see a small, thin woman with a mass of long, curling gray hair. She is smiling; four missing front teeth don't stop her from smiling. She is talking, she cannot stop talking. In her excitement and happiness, she cannot keep still. She sits, she stands, she wants to know everything. She pulls me to the kitchen to make tea. The apartment is as I knew it would be, bare, dusty, a broken bed propped against a bedroom wall, the crack in the kitchen wall, and there they still are, the scuttling cockroaches. We talk. We go to a nearby café; she hungrily eats a plate of fatty pork that I cannot bear to touch, and we wrap up my portion to take home for her dinner. We pass an old beggar woman, and Liya gives her a coin. Back in the apartment, we drink more tea. She opens a bureau drawer and takes out heaps of yellowing photographs, brittle papers, books. She piles them in my lap. I look at the books. I am astonished. *My* books. I look at the photographs. *My* life: a baby in my mother's arms, a little girl holding my father's hand, an adolescent with my cousins, my darling aunts and uncles, my clean, comfortable house, my sweet mother, my wedding day, my full life. What did Liya think as year after year her cousin's life was placed before her? Did she see what I see now? Did she see my great, good, pure dumb luck? Did she see that my road had always been clear and open before me? Why didn't *I* know that?

ACKNOWLEDGMENTS

I am surely debt-ridden: in a literary way, especially to the late Sergei Dovlatov, for his small (in length) masterpiece, "Ours." For inspiriting words, to say nothing of generous deeds, I owe more than I can say to Richard Poirer, Michael Train, Richard Howard, Craig Raine, Elsa and Norman Rush, Kitty Ross, David Alexander, Lucretia Stewart, Vivian Mazur, Barbara Levoy, Jenny Snider, Leah Gardner, Ed and Nancy Sorel, Anna Hamburger, Helene Pleasants, the late Jean Evans, George and Edith Penty, John Bowers, Sylvia Plachy. Many thanks to my agent, Georges Borchardt.

The stories in *How I Came Into My Inheritance* are drawn from the once-upon-a-time in the common life of my family when we clustered as closely as bees in a hive. Now we are scattered and few. My cousins have their own stories, which would surely be otherwise. I hope they will indulge me in mine.

My thanks to Alex Dunai, an exemplary historian and guide to Ukraine, and to Daniel Mendelsohn, who put me in touch with him. Alya Kashper responded to alarms about the well-being of my cousin, Liya Alexandrovna, in Moscow, and also served as my translator in that city. I couldn't have wished for a more congenial traveling companion than my cousin Vivian Mazur.

I am indebted to many scholars of Soviet and Ukranian history: Robert Conquest, Orlando Figes, Anna Reid, and Vitaly Shentalinsky, to name just a few.

Our household wouldn't function without the help of Gilda Caverte and Avelino Caverte, and I thank them from my heart. Now, and always, I am deeply grateful to my first readers, my husband, Ben Sonnenberg, and our friend Michael Train. My friend and editor, Daniel Menaker, is the best of his kind, in both departments.

ABOUT THE AUTHOR

DOROTHY GALLAGHER was born and raised in New York City. She was a features editor for *Redbook* magazine and then became a freelance writer. Her work has been published in *The New York Times Magazine*, *The New York Times Book Review*, and *Grand Street*. Her previous books are *Hannah's Daughters*, an account of a six-generation matrilineal family; and *All the Right Enemies*, a biography of the Italian-American anarchist Carlo Tresca. She lives in New York with her husband, the writer Ben Sonnenberg.